The New Immigration: A Challenge to American Society

THE NEW IMMIGRATION:

A CHALLENGE TO AMERICAN SOCIETY

NATHAN GLAZER

Third Distinguished Graduate Research Lecture
San Diego State University

San Diego State University Press

Library of Congress Cataloging-in-Publication Data

Glazer, Nathan.
  The new immigration.

  (Distinguished graduate research lecture ; 3rd)
  Lecture delivered Mar. 14, 1984.
  Bibliography: p.
  Includes index.
  1. United States—Emigration and immigration.
2. Immigrants—United States.   I. Title.   II. Series.
JV6455.5.G42   1988   325.73   87-32229

ISBN 0-916304-81-7

Contents

The Distinguished Graduate Research Lecture Series

The Distinguished Graduate Research Lecture Series of San Diego State University brings eminent scientists and scholars of national and international status to the campus to present "all-University" graduate colloquia on generic problems of research and graduate education. These colloquia combine open lectures of general interest with smaller seminars and workshops for the graduate students and faculty who are actively pursuing research in areas related to the colloquia topics. The series is sponsored by the Graduate Division and Research and the University Research Council, and is supported in part through Instructionally Related Activities Funds. Each academic discipline or department which offers a graduate degree at San Diego State University may nominate notable scholars to participate in the series. Exposure to and interaction with such distinguished researchers is an integral part of the instructional experience for all graduate students at San Diego State University. Each of the lectures in the series will be published to assure their increased availability to the students and faculty of the University, and to the community at large. This book, *The New Immigration: A Challenge to American Society*, originated as the Third San Diego State University Distinguished Graduate Research Lecture.

Nathan Glazer: A Biographical Sketch

Nathan Glazer was born February 25, 1923 in New York City, the son of Depression-era parents and one of a family of seven children. After finishing high school in the Bronx, he entered the City College of New York and eventually became a sociology major, graduating with a Phi Beta Kappa key in 1944. He obtained a master's degree in linguistics and anthropology in the same year at the University of Pennsylvania after working in an accelerated course designed to train linguists for the US Army.

Active in Jewish organizations, he was at that time, by his own description, "socialist." Raised in the Depression, he never expected to work where he wanted—in an academic institution. "No one I knew had ever held an academic job," he recalled; but he believed he could write, so he looked for a position on a labor newspaper. One can only admire his perspicacity in preparing for such practical employment by doing his master's thesis on Swahili—an East African language. Instead, he did begin what was to be a distinguished writing career as an assistant editor of *Commentary* and studied evenings for his doctorate from Columbia. It is apparently not recorded what the Graduate Dean at Columbia thought of editor Glazer when he noted (he must have noted) that he took seventeen years to finish the doctorate.

But what seventeen years those must have been! He collaborated and published with the renowned scholar David Reisman at Yale on the changing nature of our national character. He participated in an editorial capacity in two publishing houses and lectured at UC Berkeley, the University of Chicago, and Bennington and Smith Colleges. He was a Guggenheim Fellow in 1954, he also wrote or co-authored (or edited) four major works—all of this before his 1962 doctorate!

The Lonely Crowd in which Fellow Glazer collaborated with David Riesman and Paul Denney at MIT, has been called one of the best and most influential works of descriptive sociology published in the United States in the twentieth century, and his work with Daniel Patrick Moynihan, *Beyond the Melting Pot*, has become a standard text in sociology classes throughout the country.

Positive and optimistic in his approach, and with extraordinary energy, he has researched and written on racial matters during times when such commentary was not popular nor always appreciated. "It was almost impossible" author Glazer said of the 1960s and 1970s, "for either blacks or whites to discuss racial matters. The facts were known, but significant research almost ceased and analysis was dumb."

A professor of Sociology at UC Berkeley during 1963-69, Glazer was appointed the first professor of Education and Social Structure at Harvard in 1969, a position he holds today. He has been honored as an invited lecturer and with honorary doctorates at numerous institutions. He has demonstrated and reinforced the value of research and inquiry, not only in secluded libraries, but in the controversial social arena of the day.

1

THE NEW IMMIGRATION: A CHALLENGE TO AMERICAN SOCIETY

I have taken the problem of the New American Immigration, and it raises questions which are truly perplexing and presents to us a situation which I believe is unique in American society. The question it raises, which I will come to in the course of my lecture, is as to the political capacity of American society and American government, as to whether a problem which deeply influences American society and will shape us for the future, can really be dealt with by our present political institutions. That sounds serious, but I will hope to defend that position.

Let me describe the situation which I know I have presented slightly sensationally, in a somewhat unsensational way, with a bit of background. America is an immigration society or has been an immigration society, but in 1924 we decided—by "we" I mean we as a nation using our political institutions—to put a stop to mass immigration to this country. I will not defend that decision. In fact, I was among those, when I became conscious, who fought against it. But it is true, that for a long time, a very heavy immigration had flowed to this country. Between 1900 and 1914 immigration to this country, at that time almost entirely from Europe—immigration from Asia having been stopped by legislation in the 1880s affecting China and by the gentlemen's agreement of 1906 affecting Japan—was flowing about a million a year; we had less than half the number of people we have today. The World War stopped immigration for a while obviously because people couldn't come. Immigration then resumed in a flood after the war and reached very high figures in the early '20s. At that time, a major debate was continuing in the country, a debate which had started at least 20 or 30 years before, as to whether the United States should remain a country of basically uncontrolled immigration in which any European (or basically European), who wished to enter the country—or any person from the Western Hemisphere, where there were also no restrictions—could. The debate was largely shaped by the character of the immigration at that time, which was Catholic and Jewish, Southern European and East European, the two largest streams being Italian and East European Jewish. The end of the debate was the imposition of a quota system in which each European country was given a quota limiting how many people it could send to this country each year and in which, in effect, mass immigration from Europe came to an end.

The fact is, between 1924 and 1945 there was almost no immigration to this country, almost none if we compare it to the historical record when it had been so heavy. In the later '20s the Quota Act took its toll, then the depression began and nobody wanted to come; then WWII came and nobody could come, so for a long time American public opinion lived in the consciousness and expectation that America was completed.

When I first began to write about ethnic and immigrant issues, and I believe my first articles were in the mid-1940s, I also took that position. If one studied immigration and ethnicity, one was studying communities that had been created in the past and were undergoing various changes. No one expected that America would again become an immigration society. If you doubt that expectation of the '40s and '50s, you can look back at the record and look at those who were writing about it. Immigration was something for historians to study. The Quota Act of 1924, which was modified slightly by the McCarran Act in 1954, controlled immigration. The consensus in American immigration that we wanted no more people in the United States can be underlined and documented by a story which is familiar to some of you, and about which more and more books are being written: the case of Jewish refugees from Germany and occupied Europe.

The fact was that these refugees, if they came from Poland where the great majority of Jews lived in Europe, were not eligible to come to this country except under the Polish quota, which was not very large. Despite the fact that President Roosevelt was considered sympathetic to the problem of the Jewish refugees whose fate in the end was death, despite the fact that we have in this country a large Jewish community believed to be very influential, no modification of those restrictions existed until the end of the war. Even proposals to bring in a thousand Jewish orphans under parole, who would then be sent back out of the country at the end of the war, were turned down. This was the strength of the consensus, and I call it a consensus because today we would want to call it the expression of American racism and ethnocentrism and, in good measure, it was. We know that American officials in the State Department, who were anti-Semitic or opposed to immigration, argued that refugees would include Nazi agents, Communist agents—anyone, as long as they could maintain their position that no one should be let in.

But if you look at another aspect of the story which is now being studied in some depth by American Jewish scholars, you will see that even the American Jewish community partly shared the consensus and refused to take the kinds of actions which today are simply normal, and not only the Jewish community but other ethnic and immigrant communities, in defending the interests of compatriots, family members and so on. The Jewish community was remarkably quiescent, although not entirely, in pushing for relaxation of immigration laws. I might also point out that at the time there were more Jewish Congressmen than there are today Hispanic American Congressmen, but they were politically less powerful. Recall that House Speaker O'Neill said he would not bring to a vote the proposed immigration legislation which I will discuss, the Simpson-Mazzoli Act, because, among other reasons, of the opposition of Hispanic American Congressmen. An action like that simply was not conceivable in the middle '40s, even though some Jewish Congressmen like Emanuel Seller and others held very important positions. The point I want to make is that the consensus was a strong one. It is true that after 1945 immigration did resume in a modest way, under the Immigration Act of '24 and under special legislation which allowed in a few hundred thousand displaced persons, Jews and non-Jews, from Eastern Europe.

Immigration in the '50s was on the order of magnitude of 200,000 to 250,000 a year, considerably more than it had been in the '30s or '40s but still remarkably modest. We lived with the Quota Act of 1924, embarrassed to some extent at the racist attitudes embodied in it. That is a little strong, but there were racist aspects to it, certainly in that no Asians could enter under it. We modified it a little in 1952. Many American Congressmen, as the children of the new immigrants became more important politically, attacked the Act and in 1965 a new consensus emerged and a new immigration act was passed. This is an act that owes a great deal to the work of Senator John F. Kennedy, who later became President. It was passed after his death and also owes a great deal to the work of Senator Edward Kennedy.

The Act reflects the views of the older new immigrants, that is to say the people who had been coming in the 1920s and whose entry was stopped more or less by the Immigration Act of 1924. The new Act eliminated the quotas based on the assumption that the composition of the American population should not change. This is a most interesting story. It involved many historians and sociologists because the Act required someone, and it was a body of scholars who did, to figure out what proportion of the American population in 1920 had been contributed to by each European country. On that basis, therefore, Italy got its 1200, Poland its 2200, Germany its 20,000, England its 40,000, Ireland its 30,000 and so on. In other words, a point I perhaps I did not stress efficiently when I said earlier that we thought America was completed in 1944, the Immigration Act's intention was to freeze the proportions of the American population—a utopian and unlikely prospect—by limiting immigration in proportion to some estimate of what each country had contributed since the beginnings of the history of our country to the American population. As I say, that Act went into oblivion.

In 1965, a new act was passed in which we did not discriminate among countries as to how many each could send—each was allowed 20,000—and in which the major emphasis of immigration in the future was to be reunification of families. It was an act whose muscle was provided by the children of Jewish and Italian immigrants and by Jewish organizations because these were the communities that had been created by immigration, and they saw that they believed in immigration; they believed the future of America demanded more immigration.

As a result of the 1965 Act two things happened that no one expected. One thing was that immigration shifted sharply from Europe to Asia and Latin America. This is not because a lot of Europeans could not continue to come if they wanted to—each European country had a quota of 20,000; it's because Europeans had by that time become prosperous. Despite the fact that their distant cousins in the United States had pushed through this reform to permit more Irish, English, Germans, Poles, Italians and others to come, they stopped coming.

On the other hand, since this Act did not have any restrictions on the basis of race or continent, people from Asia and Latin America began to come. Those are the ones that wanted to come. The second unexpected thing was for the first time in a substantial way, a major part of American immigration became illegal, undocumented, or in any case uncontrolled. Obviously, we could not have had much illegal immigration before 1924—there was not much that could be illegal unless you were Chinese or Japanese, and it's true they were smuggled in. But, under the Act of 1965, we thought we had accommodated all the interests of those who wanted to come. We thought we had modified the way we wanted to complete America by giving a larger share to the immigrants of 1880 to 1920, the Catholic and Jewish immigrants, but it turns out they were not the beneficiaries of the Act. They were not the ones who were interested in coming; new streams of population came.

The fact is, the Act of 1965, which was expected to be the consensus upon which American immigration policy was conducted and based, had broken down by the middle '70s. Everyone knew there was a substantial stream of uncontrolled immigration from a number of countries, but primarily Mexico, which shares its long frontier right near us, and we began thinking of what we could do about it. The fact is, we haven't figured out what to do about it since we started thinking about it. President Carter set up a distinguished select commission on immigration which Father Hesberg of Notre Dame chaired. It conducted excellent research under the guidance of Lawrence Fuchs of Brandeis and came out with what it hoped was a proposal shortly before President Reagan took office.

President Reagan's administration has made various proposals, and these proposals and others have emerged in something called the Simpson-Mazzoli Act, which again and again fails to find passage in Congress. The interesting situation is that we are more and more buffeted by actions of others that we cannot control. We cannot prevent Castro from expelling 100,000 Cubans if he wants to; he may try again. We cannot prevent Vietnam from expelling hundreds of thousands of its Chinese and dissident population. We cannot prevent easily, though we are trying, large numbers of Haitians coming here to escape the poorest country in the Western Hemisphere. We cannot prevent civil war in El Salvador from leading to hundreds of thousands to decide to find a better life here, or revolutions in Nicaragua leading many more to come, and we can apparently not prevent a very large stream of undocumented immigrants from Mexico.

Now, we should ask the question, a fair question, why worry? That's a very good question; I've pondered it. There are two classic positions on immigration. One is the "don't worry" position and the other is the "worry very much" position and neither of them, I think, have much support today. The first position is the liberal position. It is the position that we are a country of immigrants, we are all the children of immigrants; we have been made great by immigration and further immigration will continue to make us great. I don't think that's the position that most of Congress adheres to or most of the American population adheres to. We do know that if you ask, should we do more to control immigration? about 75 percent or 80 percent of the American people say yes. By the way, roughly the same percentage of Mexicans say yes, so everyone feels it's right. We're a sovereign nation; we should be able to control our borders; we should be able to make decisions as to who becomes an American, who doesn't; who has the right to work here, who doesn't, and so on. The interesting thing is that every other nation takes the same position, too. We are a world of sovereign nations.

The conservative position has always been that we want less people rather than more; we don't want people of different cultures, different religions, different races. Let me propose to you, since it's common to believe the conservatives now in control are reactionaries, that position isn't playing much of a role today in discussions on immigration. If you look at the debates on Simpson-Mazzoli, if you look at the editorials written in the newspapers, hardly anyone—almost no one—says that the people of the wrong race are entering, or people of the wrong religion are entering, or people who are not going to become good Americans. That's really not playing much of a role in the argument. Maybe many people feel that underneath, but we are by now a country in which it is very unpopular to express judgements as to ethnic groups, races, and so on, and we will see very little discussion on that.

That argument over immigration today, the real argument, the arguments taking place in the press, in the Congress, among experts and so on, breaks down completely if you try to interpret it in liberal or conservative terms. Let me describe to you who are the groups that have prevented—a lot of the forces that have prevented—up to now an attempt at more effective immigration control from passage in Congress, and they are a very strange mixture which explains why the ordinary or the expected liberal-conservative breakdown on most issues just doesn't work. Against strong immigration control, we, of course, have employers of undocumented aliens or employers of landed immigrants with green cards or new immigrants. Basically this is not so new, because even in the old debate of the 1920s, the Chamber of Commerce did not like the idea of immigration control. If you employ labor, you want more of it. If there is more of it, the price of labor will go down. You can make other arguments.

There is a second group which is not exactly employers who are against the new immigration controls that are being proposed and whom I might call the ideologists of the free market. I would hazard a guess that the strongest editorials written against the Simpson-Mazzoli Act, and against the attempt to control undocumented immigration to this country, have appeared in the *Wall Street Journal*. I do not know how widely the *Wall Street Journal* is read here; but it does have, as you may know, the largest circulation of any newspaper in the country, and it's possible that its editorial page is the most influential in the country. The *Wall Street Journal* is against immigration control, you might say, because it is the voice of the employers. Therefore, it wants more workers who will work for less wages rather than fewer workers who will then permit the remaining workers to ask for more wages, but its major position is really an ideological free market position. It says people come here to work, if there wasn't work here they wouldn't come here. They are against State interference with most things, they are against State regulation of almost anything you can think of, and to them the control of people is as bad as the control of Japanese cars. Just as free trade is good, free movement of people is good. That is the position of the *Wall Street Journal*.

Up to now I've described two elements: employers who have an interest in more labor and ideologists of the free market. There is a third group which normally is not allied with the first two. The supporters of civil liberties are against the new efforts to control immigration because these efforts propose a system of national registration. This is the kind of system that exists all over Europe and obviously all over other countries in which people are forced to carry on them, or are expected to carry on them, papers indicating their legal status. Civil libertarians are against this because they are against the notion of everybody being put into a computer and being tracked; supporters of the interests of Hispanic Americans are against it because they believe Hispanic Americans will be stopped on the street and be asked to show their papers. Another reason civil libertarians can be very clearly placed among the opponents of stricter immigration controls or controlled immigration is that they believe in human rights, and they propose many measures which make it impossible to really control immigration. These measures include rights to hearing, rights not to be stopped in the street, rights not to be asked if you are here legally, and so on.

There's a fourth group—and I must say here I am not quite clear where it stands—and that is the Mexican American and Hispanic American political leadership which on the whole is also critical of immigration control. It is critical not because it feels immigration controls are directed not against Mexican Americans—they're all here—but against the others in Mexico who might come and thus might be used as a form of discrimination against Hispanic Americans here.

Who is for immigration control? In theory, as I said, 70 to 80 percent of the American population and, if you were to poll them individually, perhaps a majority of members of Congress. Administrators are for it, the ones who are responsible for this problem, and they feel that it is out of control. Some trade unions are for it. The trade unions have not played the most active role, but normally trade unions want fewer workers rather than more workers because that increases the price of labor, or one hopes it does. Blacks are for more immigration control, but they have not played a major role in this issue. Though you would think from the point of view of the interests of Blacks, competition for low-wage jobs in areas where they have worked or could work might be serious. I will propose that one of the reasons Black leadership has not played such a big role in the fight against the flow of undocumented immigration may be that they are no longer interested in whether Blacks can or cannot work in hotels, or as dishwashers in restaurants, or as pickers of agricultural crops. The Black leadership hopes for better jobs for Blacks, and maybe they are right. In any case, they have not played a major role in this issue.

10

As in the case of so many issues, this is the kind of issue in which minorities with strong interests and strong passions are able to control the issue against the majority, which doesn't feel that strongly about it; it isn't committed to it that much. The minorities, I have said, are the employers, the ideologists of the free market, the civil libertarians, Hispanic American leadership. The majority is everyone else who thinks we should have an immigration policy, but small groups with strong feelings can generally outweigh large groups without strong feelings.

Is this the sort of issue that can be settled by analysis? I have said, "Why worry?" Is this a sort of issue in which we can say, through analysis, what is best for America? Well, when I began my reading and writing and thinking for this presentation, I was sure I would come to a good answer, but I must say I haven't. There are three kinds of arguments that are discussed about immigration—discussed in the past, discussed today. And I would like to say a few words about each of them. One kind is the economic argument; it seems the easiest. One can always figure out if something will be better for the country or worse for the country; will it increase the Gross National Product or will it not? The fact is there have been rather good efforts to analyze the economic effects of immigration and we do not really have an answer. If you want to say it's good, you'll find support. If you want to say it's bad, you'll also find support.

Recently, there have been two studies of a narrow aspect of this issue: What is the cost of immigration in social services in California; and what is the cost of immigration in social services in Texas? I will not go through the elaborate methodology of how you figure out what an immigrant costs, but you figure out if he's going to school, and that costs so much, and if he goes to the hospital, that costs something else, and if he gets welfare, that costs something else. It came out that California loses a little bit on immigration and Texas gains a little bit on immigration. Not surprising when you consider that California has very good social services and Texas has much worse social services.

However social services were only a very small part of the analysis. At least the California analysis, conducted by Tom Muller of the Urban Institute in a volume called *The Fourth Wave and the Impact of Immigration on Southern California*, which I understand has already created a little bit of controversy in California, points out that these are only the beginning costs. For example, there are certain industries that wouldn't exist if you did not have low wage labor. Now you have to raise the question: Does the existence of that low wage labor industry—clothing, toy manufacturing, or something in plastics—does it benefit California or does it hurt California? Would it be better for California if employers could not find cheap labor, and therefore went out of business, and let that product be manufactured in Korea or Mexico, or is it better for California that it has low wage labor, that industry exists, and therefore California has more taxes, and so on? Tom Muller even tried to figure out: Does Mexican immigration hurt or help Blacks? A most elaborate set of regressions demonstrated that it helps Blacks a little. How could you explain that? Because Mexican immigration in California provides a need for more social services—nurses and social welfare workers, teachers, and so on—and that's the kind of fields a lot of Blacks are going into, so more of them are employed than otherwise. I go into this not to make an argument that we can settle the issue of immigration through economic effects; almost to say we can't. At least my reading the economists has led me to conclude that I can't say what the overall judgement is. That, I think, is a conservative position, because most people like to say immigration must be good for the country and I really am not sure. If there were fewer immigrants, would wages be higher, would there be more labor-saving machinery employed, who knows? But I'm not saying it's bad for the country, either.

There's a second kind of argument which has played a very important role in debates on immigration, but not so much anymore, these are cultural arguments. I think these are also ambiguous. In the late 19th century, some of America's leading intellectuals, like Henry Adams and Henry James, were convinced immigration was bad for the country. Henry James, writing in his *American Scene* of his return to America has many passages describing—I don't know the right term for someone who is lifting up his skirts so as not to have them stained by other people—but describing his distance from the new immigrants that were crowding American cities, such as Boston, New York, and so on. Henry Adams took a much stronger position. He said the America that his great-grandfather and grandfather had created was being destroyed. Many people believed that at that time an authentic American culture was being destroyed. I don't think we believe that anymore. Now many of us think immigrants added to it, made it richer. But there is no argument that can be extrapolated forever. If you take the position that American culture was provincial in the mid-nineteenth century, became richer and more cosmopolitan in the mid-twentieth century because of immigration, are you going to take the position it can become even richer and more cosmopolitan as the rest of the world comes in? At some point there are losses, and there are felt losses. These are things that are extremely hard to explicate, but is the kind of thing that happens when people say, "my old neighborhood isn't like it used to be anymore," and "I don't like it, it's different." Maybe it's simply nostalgia for what one knew, but it is true that many countries do take the position that there is an authentic stream of culture which would be modified beyond recognition if streams of immigration of other sources were to reach certain sizes.

Germans are very worried. We don't take Germans seriously perhaps, but they're very worried by the fact that they now have, in a country of more than 60 million or 70 million, 2 million foreigners. We wouldn't consider that very serious. The French are very worried. In a country of 50 million, they have 2 million foreigners. But at some point, one might well understand that a Frenchman might feel that if a great number of

Moslems raising mosques, that France would no longer be the France they knew and recognized. Now, I don't know how you want to value that. I don't know how you want to value the sense of a known country. I refer to names which are still in measure respected, like Henry James and Henry Adams, to point out that at one time there were Americans, lecturers, who took this seriously in the 1920s, many, particularly Anglo-American ones who were opponents of immigration. We don't hear about that now.

A final measure—as I pointed out there's no answer on the cultural side, either—the "Why worry?" side. On the political side, in the past, much of the concern about immigration has been over loyalty. I won't go through that history. The loyalty of Germans in World War I; the loyalty of Japanese in World War II. Maybe those were misguided concerns, but there was a sense that, as the country becomes more diverse, its ability not to be a badly divided country would be in danger. In other words, some degree of commonality was a good idea, and limitation of the extremes of immigration was one way to achieve it. I don't think any of these three arguments gives us an answer. I think that the only element that is a proper basis for concern about this issue is the reality that a major force changing American society is now out of the control of American political institutions. In other words, whether you think immigration is good or bad; whether you think 500,000 people should enter the country a year, as roughly we have now, or 800,000 as occurred in 1980, or a million, if you include illegal immigration; whether you think we should have more Asians, or more Latin Americans, or more Europeans, the fact is that whatever you think, we do not have any policies today that can implement what we feel would be the image of the country we want.

Now we'll have discussion, and you might answer, we should not have any image of the country. The country should be the country envisaged by the *Wall Street Journal*, the one that exists on the basis of who wants to come, and who wants to leave, and what the economic opportunities are. Maybe that's the answer, I'm not sure. But the fact is, today immigration is not under control. More seriously, we cannot create the measures that might bring it under control and might express whatever that national desire, or national will, might be.

I will describe our recent efforts to forge a consensus and where it stands today. The consensus that we're trying to forge is the Simpson-Mazzoli Act, named after Senator Simpson and Congressman Mazzoli which is in no sense original. This is not to criticize them: it is based on the consensus of all the studies we have been undertaking since the mid-'70s. It is exactly the kind of act, more or less, that could have emerged from the select commission appointed by a Democratic administration, and it's the kind of act that this administration is supporting. So there is a kind of consensus of informed opinion. The Act is based on a compromise which is itself based on what we might call a new humanitarianism and liberalism, which is the common norm of American life today. It is not a 1924 Act. It is not a restrictive act.

The nature of the Act is as follows, and it has two major measures. One measure is amnesty for those who are here, a very important measure: we don't know how many are here. Some commissioners of immigration claim 12 million, which everyone now agrees is excessive and others have said 2 million which everyone says is too little. For some reason, the consensus seems to have come around to the figure of about 4 million, and maybe 6 million. It is inconceivable that the United States we know can expel 4 million people. We are not Nigeria which not long ago expelled a million Ghanians. We wouldn't do it. They have wives, children, jobs, and so on, so the first notion is amnesty. I won't even go into the details which Congress has debated, left and right, of when amnesty goes into effect; that is, how long do you have to have been here to be eligible for amnesty? Because if all you do is talk about amnesty for those who are here, you simply encourage more and more people to come to get in under amnesty, so there has to be a cut-off date. Some Congressmen say 1981, some say 1980, and some say 1983, and so on. At any rate, the first measure is amnesty. To say, "okay, let's clear the books, you're here," that's all right.

The next measure is control, but a very interesting form of control which I think is worth thinking about. I don't mean control at the border, which, again, I think would conflict with our sense of the kind of country we want. We don't want a border with barbed wire and guard dogs, etc. In a way, it sort of suits the American spirit that the border is sort of open, and we don't really want to really close it down. So the issue is control through employers. Very ingenious. After all, who is the friend of employers? We won't have the border patrol try to keep you out, or the Department of State and the visa people. We'll leave it up to the businessmen. That will keep them out. If you don't hire them, they won't come. If you do hire them, we'll fine you. That's basically the compromise of Simpson-Mazzoli. Will it work? Well, you'll have to think it through. I think it won't, and I think that most informed people writing about immigration don't think it will. I refer to an article by Tom Harwood in a magazine I edit, *The Public Interest* and to a book by John Crewdson, *The Tarnished Door*. The reasons most people don't think it will work are the reasons you might think about. Many of the employers of undocumented immigrants will not be found. Many of them have political influence and will not be fined. Many of them will be able to argue they didn't know. Interestingly enough, even though the employer is supposed to be responsible for hiring someone who does not have papers, people will not be required to have papers because the Civil Liberties Union and the Mexican-American community are against that. So it will be up to the employer to try to figure out, without possessing the resources of the Immigration and Naturalization Service, whether the person he is hiring is really an illegal immigrant. If you think it through, it just won't work.

Let me conclude. The issue I have argued is not a liberal-conservative issue. I think more and more issues are not liberal-conservative issues. It is an issue which, by an accident of history, a rich country, the United States, lives next to a poor big country, Mexico. That's not the only issue, but that's the main issue. And that's a peculiar situation, peculiar only because it exists nowhere else in the world. Nowhere else in the world is there a land border between the developed world and the developing world. If there isn't a land border, you can control immigration because people have to come by sea, and airplanes, and so on. That is the issue we deal with. It is certainly changing the United States and will continue to change the United States. Mexico has about one third the population of the United States and its natural growth, in absolute figures, is about that of the United States each year. As more and more immigrants come, as we know if we are students of immigration, more and more want to come. It takes the first to tell you that life here is not so bad, or you can manage, or we can put you up, or we can help you out. And the time will come when the source of immigration from Mexico will reach further and further into the society as more and more knowledge about the United States spreads into the society as more and more knowledge is created through the mass media and through word of mouth.

I began this talk, and I began thinking about this talk, with a kind of over-confidence that I would propose something at the end. I've decided I don't have anything to propose at the end. There have recently been some excellent analysts of the situation. I mentioned Crewdson, and I should mention Tom Fallows in the *Atlantic*, and they have decided that:

1) nothing can be done, and

2) if nothing can be done, there is nothing to worry about.

I disagree with the second point, but I suspect they're right about the first point. Thank you.

2

COLLOQUIUM

The material in this chapter is extracted from the comments and responses by Professor Glazer at the research coloquium which followed his formal lecture at San Diego State University, March 14, 1984.

Feinberg:

This colloquium is one of a number of events scheduled in conjunction with the Distinguished Graduate Research Lecture. The lecture is one of a series that has been sponsored by the University Research Council and by the Graduate Division.

This colloquium is really designed to be a less formal presentation—an opportunity for the faculty and for graduate students to interact with Professor Glazer. I want to acknowledge the efforts of our host departments, the Department of Sociology and the Department of Policy Studies and Bilingual Cross-Cultural Education which used to be the Multi-Cultural Education Department.

I want now to turn over the proceedings to Professor John Weeks who is the chair of the Sociology Department, and ask him to introduce our guest today.

Professor Weeks:

Thank you. It was nineteen years ago, in the spring of 1965, that I first met Professor Glazer. He was a professor of sociology at UC Berkeley and I was a young and timid undergraduate, eager to take a class from a man whose works had been rather prominently featured in several other sociology courses that I had already taken at Berkeley. So I signed up for his Urban Sociology class, and in truth I was not disappointed. It was a very stimulating class, a very good class, and despite the fact that his reader had given me a B on a paper, after discussion with Professor Glazer the grade was raised to an A and I still appreciate that. I went on to specialize in demography and our paths didn't cross much after that, but I can tell you that on numerous occasions I did see Professor Glazer leaving campus at Berkeley with one hand on the steering wheel, the other hand on a book and, so far as I could tell, neither eye on the road. I would have made a bet for any amount of money in those years that he would never arrive at age sixty-one with those kinds of driving habits. But unfortunately for me, I didn't make any such bets, and fortunately for us he is still around stirring up a lot of controversy, stimulating ideas within the academic community. It's with a great deal of pleasure that I introduce to you Professor Nathan Glazer of Harvard.

Professor Glazer:

I want to make a few more introductory remarks and then I will read you a part of a paper I haven't published, which I think raises an interesting, complicated question. By the way, Mr. Weeks' introduction reminded me of another immigration story. I recently reviewed in the *Boston Globe*, not a major national newspaper, a book on immigration by John Crewdson called *The Tarnished Door*, this kind of thing we're going to be hearing more and more about. Mr. Crewdson is a Pulitzer Prize-winning journalist. He had written a series on undocumented immigration for the *New York Times*, and is now an editor for the *Chicago Sun Times*.

I got a rather nice letter from him saying, "Thank you for my review. It makes up for the B you gave me in Berkeley twenty years ago!" It was another one of those classes where there were I don't know how many students and I never trusted the teaching assistant system. Sociology, as one engineering student once said to another in a class of a thousand I was lecturing to, is a field in which there are no right answers. Which means that sometimes the teaching assistant will give you a B and the professor feels it's worth an A, and sometimes the reverse. If it's the reverse, of course, you don't come and ask him so you'll never know.

Now, on to my topic, and I want to make a few introductory remarks. The Southwest is now the major port of immigration into the United States. We have immigrants in Boston; New York City is still playing a substantial role, but American immigration is now statistically more than four-fifths Asian and Latin American. European immigration is more modest. Inevitably, attention is focused on the Southwest, from Texas to California; inevitably, very strongly on Southern California. Indeed, Southern California reminds me, or it should remind one, of New York in 1910, with a million immigrants a year coming in. As far as the absolute figures go, California falls short of that, but possibly not that much short. It's true that a lot of immigrants are going back, too. It's a very complex situation.

The question is raised that I think we—as sociologists, political scientists and social scientists—are wont to think about and do think about. Do we expect, or do we have reason to expect, that the pattern of Mexican-American immigration and assimilation in this country will be similar of that of previous immigrant groups, which have been primarily European groups?

I want to raise some considerations which might lead one to say it's hardly likely it will be the same. Something different is going to happen. I sense that a lot of Americans feel that something different is going to happen, and that is the reason for a kind of concern—concern which is definitely now below the surface, but reminds one of the anti-immigration sentiment, agitation, and organization of the 1920s when the Ku Klux Klan was active. When Italian, Jewish and East European groups were proportionately as large as the current Mexican-American population, they didn't dare to raise a voice against what became the most radical restriction of immigration in American history. It is a different period.

But under the surface I sense there is a concern that something different is going to happen. I'm going to read you some of my paper, written from this perspective as to why there is this concern and whether we have any reason to take it seriously. Do we expect something different? If something is different, is this something that is dangerous to the degree of unity that we have come to expect in American society, politics, and in the projection of American ideals and interests in the world? That is the question that lies just barely beneath the surface that concerns most Americans, even if not directly expressed. It is sometimes expressed forcefully, as in Senator Hayakawa's efforts, now taken up by a group called U.S. English, to make English the national language of the United States. We can also see this concern expressed in the activities of a relatively small group, the Federation for American Immigration Reform, which wants to restrict immigration, in contrast to the Simpson-Mazzoli Act, which is only an effort to create a national consensus on controlling immigration. But I do think this concern affects more than these groups.

Now, what is the common understanding as to the political career of immigrant ethnic groups in the United States? I think that it's against that contrast that the concern is expressed. The model that we first of all seem to have is for large groups. We have political studies of the Irish, Jews, Italians, and the nineteenth-century Germans. There are many smaller groups, sometimes important locally. Among the smaller groups, Greeks have been remarkably successful politically. In Massachusetts, where there are not many Greeks, the last [1980] census which, as some of you know asked for census identification, came up with 70,000 Greeks for Massachusetts. A mere fragment for a big state, nevertheless, we now have a Greek-origin governor and a Greek-origin senator. We have had a Greek-origin vice president. I mention this, by the way, to point out that group size does not necessarily correlate with political success.

But the general focus of our studies and our concerns is on large groups, understandably. It is they that can swing some weight. What is large? If we take Jews as the smallest of the large groups I have mentioned, it is five or six million. Such groups may have national influence, as well as marked local influence in different parts of the country. It is our common understanding of how those groups operate politically that raises questions about Mexican-Americans. Is that group to become acculturated to American politics; organizing around the combination of interests that are general and affect all people in a given economic or occupational situation, as well as interests specific to the group? That's our general understanding of the assimilation of ethnic groups into American politics. They always have a mix of interests.

For example, the Irish, who have been by far the most successful ethnic group in politics, reflect this mix of interests. On the one hand, the Irish, originally poor and uneducated urban laborers in the middle nineteenth century, were concerned with their economic situation and that was the concern of their leaders. Entering politics in the mid and later nineteenth century when public social policies did not really exist in this country, they expressed their general interest by attempting to control the jobs that local political government could control, the jobs that the "machine" could give out. The specific Irish interests were more sharply defined against Protestant control of the schools, for support of Ireland's struggle for independence against England, against England in general, and against prohibition.

This mix of the general and the ethnic, or the class-and interest-based, and the value- and emotion-based issues, is characteristic of all ethnic groups. At a later time, when government was becoming involved in protecting the interests of working men, Irish political leaders like Al Smith were among the leaders in social reform. Tip O'Neill still represents this tradition (my congressman, by the way) and this mix. By now, most of the Irish have moved to the suburbs and few are poor and uneducated working men. However, the Boston area still continuously attracts Irish immigrants.

There has always been fear among longer settled groups that new immigrant groups might prove disloyal. Thus, there is a long history of efforts, for example, to suppress schools teaching in foreign languages and to limit parochial schools. These efforts reached peaks in the late 1880s, when there were laws in Illinois and Wisconsin against the schools teaching foreign languages; and in the 1920s, with laws against parochial schools in Oregon; against the teaching of German in Nebraska; and so on. The fear of disloyalty was such that German-Americans, as a distinct and self-assertive ethnic group, more or less went underground in World War I. By the time World War II came, no one even thought that German-Americans or Italian-Americans or more recent immigrants might be disloyal. That was a time when the Japanese-Americans suffered far more severely than did the Germans in World War I. So one element in the received history against which we contrast the Mexican-American situation is that, while one may be suspicious of groups at the beginning because they are new immigrants, in time all do become good Americans—acculturated, assimilated, participating fully in American politics, eschewing undue interest in the affairs of home countries.

We find a benign acceptance by other Americans of the fact that a group's interests in politics are the interests of others of their class, occupation, and region, plus some distinctive interests that arise from their ethnic status, and specifically their relationship to a homeland. I say this is a kind of benign attitude because, for example, no one much takes after the Greeks for being hostile to military aid to Turkey. We sort of accept the fact that Greeks will defend what they see as a Greek interest, even though most of their interests in politics are the interests of others of their class and status. Not everyone is benign about the fact that the Greek interest in Congress has been sufficiently strong to keep military aid to Greece (which is sort of anti-American) equal to military aid to Turkey (which is sort of pro-American). If you talk to people who are interested in the strategy of military aid, they are very annoyed about this, but there are a half-dozen Greek congressmen and senators, and they are able to maintain this balance.

This commonly accepted history of assimilation in which interest in homeland and ethnic issues declines over time while interests based on common class and occupational characteristics rise is, of course, not common for all groups. I describe what we expect in this country, rather than what has happened uniformly. There are exceptions. A single group can be seen to be so involved with a homeland interest as to raise questions of dual loyalty and, further, a potential conflict between American loyalty and loyalty to a homeland. I would say that we are now in this position — Jews have had great economic and occupational success in this country, and on the basis of this success, they are now very well represented in Congress — about eight percent or so. Since they are a group of high average age and participate vigorously as voters and contributors in politics, their over-representation is not as marked as if we take into account these additional factors. Because of their economic success, there are few domestic interests of importance that Jewish political figures must pursue for their own group. The only Jewish issue Jewish elected officials pursue tends to be that of the security of Israel. I'm not saying this is the only issue in which they're interested; I'm saying this is the only *Jewish* issue with which they tend to be involved. There aren't any other great Jewish concerns.

We find here a divergence in the common expectation that elected officials from a long-settled and successful group will have little interest in actually representing that group, rather than their district or their party. It is understandable that elected representatives of groups that are recent immigrants, poor, or recently emerged from exclusion in politics (Hispanic-Americans and Blacks) will be almost completely wrapped up with the problems of their group. Indeed, they are representatives of their group in a direct political sense in that they are almost entirely elected from districts in which their group forms a substantial majority. Few Blacks and Hispanic-Americans now represent districts in which non-Hispanic whites are numerically dominant. The Jewish representatives in Congress once also represented districts with a majority of Jews almost exclusively. In the '20s there was no Jew in Congress who did not come from a Jewish-majority district.

In recent years, such districts have declined in number; nevertheless the number of Jewish congressmen has risen. Few now run as Jews representing Jewish districts. They run as Democrats, Liberals, businessmen, lawyers—less commonly as Republicans. The same is true of congressmen of Irish origin or German origin. The common expectation is that this integration into a common political culture reduces the salience for elected officials of ethnic origin, of specific ethnic issues, and raises the importance of issues of common concern, and this is, in large measure, true.

Now, it's against this background that I want to raise some questions about Mexican-Americans. If one looks at the facts— and there are facts on Mexican-American representation in Congress, some polls, some surveys, attitudes on immigration, and so on—one does not find at this point . . . and I want to make this very clear . . . any particular divergence of Mexican-

Americans from other American ethnic groups at their point in history. One does not find, for example, any great interest in homeland issues. If you read some of the literature in 1910-1920, Mexican-Americans were arguing about the Mexican Revolution and different factions. These days one has the impression—I have gone through some of the literature—there is no particular great issue. While Mexico may be agitated when a new president comes to power, Mexican-Americans seem not to be. They seem to have no great interest, more than that of other Americans, in Latin-American issues particularly. The mayor of San Antonio, Henry Cisneros, was put on the Kissinger Commission to deal with El Salvador; whether he had any particularly greater interest in it I'm not sure. I think he was put on because President Reagan or his advisors felt that there should be one person of Mexican-American origin on the Commission. And this makes sense. Most Mexicans come from rural settings in which the sense of Mexico as a nation may be weak; others are long-settled in this country. Mexico does not seem to make any appeal to American citizens of Mexican origin to support its interests in this country. I don't think it does, in terms of Mexican consulates and so on. Yet Mexico does have these interests; they extend to trade, investment, and immigration. But one knows of no special involvement of Mexican-Americans in these issues. One suspects this is a situation not dissimilar to that of Italian-Americans in the late nineteenth and early twentieth centuries in this country, where there was no strong sense of Italy as a nation, and who, it has been suggested, became Italians rather than Apulians or Sicilians or Calabrians in this country, where they became aware of a larger identity. Perhaps something similar is true of Mexican-Americans. After all, it is not the leaders of Mexican society in politics, businessmen, and political figures, or the citizens of Mexico City who immigrate to the United States. If it were these more politicized elements, you might see something different.

But, despite this very low degree of political identification with Mexico today, it remains a troubling concern for many Americans, at least under the surface. There are a number of issues that put Mexican immigrants in a somewhat different status from the other major American immigrant groups, and I'm going to refer to five of these features which make Mexican-Americans different as a major American ethnic group.

One is that Mexico is adjacent to the United States. The second is that the territory that most Mexican-Americans live in was once Mexican, taken from Mexico in war. The third is that Mexico's economic level is far below that of the United States (and there are inevitable issues of conflict on this score such as Mexico's interest in immigration to relieve its economic problems). The fourth is that the concentration of Mexican-Americans in some cities and some sections of the country immediately adjacent to and not far from the Mexican border makes them the single dominant ethnic group in a substantial part of the Southwest. And the fifth is that conditions in the United States that facilitate assimilation—legal, political, cultural—are in certain respect less efficacious than they were during the last period of mass immigration to this country which ended in the mid-20s.

As I say, I refer to these as structural features. They do not contradict the evidence that Mexican-Americans do not diverge from the general course of acculturation and assimilation that has characterized, at different rates and with different characteristics, immigrant groups to this country. The structural realities, nevertheless, exist. I will expand briefly on each of them.

First, aside from Canada, Mexico is the only major source of American immigration directly along the land frontier. Canada has been a major source of American immigration. Many French-Canadians, in particular, settled close to the frontier; this is a point of similarity. Even in regard to the single point, there are substantial differences between Canada and Mexico as sources of immigration. Anglophone Canadians become, if they wish, almost instant Americans. There is literature on this, but this is almost a common culture, with common ethnic elements on both sides of the border, and so on. French-Canadians, despite the political ferment that now enwraps their homeland, do not reflect it. Their major period of immigration was long ago, Quebec was quiescent, and they are by now heavily acculturated and assimilated.

Second is the theme of conquered territories. No one, even the most extreme fringe elements among Mexican-Americans, demands secession and reunification. Why raise this? It is only in a small group that the question would come up. Nevertheless, the reference to this may seem ridiculous, but the fact is that we do have cases today of serious territorial claims which hope to set back decisions even older than that of the Treaty of Guadalupe Hidalgo. It is simply reality in the listing of structural features, even if it has no present consequences.

Third is the difference in the economic level between the United States and Mexico. This is possibly the most important of the features that I will discuss. It is unique. No other highly developed nation economically—not Germany, France, or the United Kingdom; not Switzerland, Belgium, or the Netherlands; not Japan—shares a long land frontier, or indeed any land frontier at all, with a developing nation which is large, rapidly growing, and making economic progress at a rate which does not give much hope of soon closing the enormous economic gap that separates it from the developed nation. This is the overwhelming factor, along with the common frontier, that raises such up-to-now insuperable problems in controlling immigration. Illegal immigration, or undocumented immigration, if you prefer the term, to European countries is nowhere as serious as it is in the United States—nowhere of the same scale (in Germany they talk of thirty to fifty thousand, or something like that), because of their geographical situation. In Japan, which gets excited about a hundred immigrants, there's none at all, legal or illegal for that matter. It's the virtue of being an island, if you want to control immigration.

The immigration issue is now the most serious one raised by this difference in economic level. It's hard to believe it will not continue to be a very major issue. One cannot see anything that will change it, not in the near future, not even in the next three or four decades. The Mexican population grows in absolute figures about as much each year as the American population, if you take natural growth, leaving out the growth in American population from immigration. But Mexico grows at a rate of about three percent a year, and it's about one-third the size of the United States, which grows at about one percent a year (natural rate of growth). This is a remarkable situation. Equally remarkable is two huge cities like Tijuana and San Diego of completely different economic levels which are practically right next to each other. There is no situation like this anywhere else in the world.

I have spoken to the immigration situation, but other issues as a result of this huge difference of economic level may come to the fore—issues involving trade and investment, issues involving the identification of Mexico with the developing world, often critical of American foreign policy. These have nowhere become significant for Mexican-Americans. Their views on immigration are not dissimilar from those of other Americans. The reality of the great difference in economic levels and the potential conflict of interest between two countries, nevertheless, exists.

Fourth is the concentration of Mexican-Americans, which is another unique feature. These elements of uniqueness have to be explained. We have had very heavy concentrations of immigrant and ethnic groups in American cities in the past, especially New York, but immigrants of one group didn't dominate a single city (perhaps with the exception of the Irish in Boston). Present-day immigration is not dominated by a single group either, but is balanced between Hispanic-Americans, dominantly Mexican-Americans, and a number of Asian groups. However, the Mexican-American is overwhelmingly the largest single immigrant group and because of its size and because of its concentration in the Southwest, it will dominate some cities and regions the way the Irish dominated Boston for generations.

With what consequences? The simple fact of concentration, one would think, delays assimilation. The fact that more than half of Los Angeles school children are now of Spanish-language background, and their concentration in typical schools is far greater than fifty percent, means that the process of language learning from English-speaking classmates is delayed, for reasons of concentration alone. Efforts to distribute school children by race and ethnic group under law and constitutional interpretation are prohibited, so desegregation has halted. We've more or less given up on that, probably for good reason. I've never been a friend at this attempt at distribution by numbers. Nevertheless, it means we will live with highly concentrated schools of Spanish-speaking children for a long time.

Concentration in schools inhibits some degree of acculturation and assimilation. In some respects, concentration may also facilitate it. Concentration offers the opportunity for political representation and political power. Political participation has an enormous potential for assimilation. If you become a politician, you're automatically an American. You're either in the state legislature or Congress, you're talking English, you're working in English , and you're working with American issues. I think politics is one of the greatest assimilatory forces in American society. It facilitates a degree of coming together of different groups that almost no other institution—neighborhood, church, school, workplace—seems capable of. Concentration, in the past, only rarely meant political minority movements, but rather participation, even if in an idiosyncratic way, in the national two-party system. But this political education and encouragement to assimilation has its limits. If Mexican-Americans come to dominate the politics of some cities—San Antonio today, Los Angeles perhaps tomorrow—with scattered opposition from the older Anglo groups and small Asian immigrant groups (who are likely, if past experience is any guide, to concentrate their efforts in education, business, and the professions; not in politics)—we may well have a situation similar to that of the dominant Irish in Boston, where politics is seen as the principal route to advancement while education and business are neglected. Indeed, smaller groups, such as the Asian groups, Greeks, Armenians, simply because their numbers do not permit dominance in politics, often place their energies in education, business, and the professions, and create a more secure base, in this manner, for later political advance. The implications of concentration and dominance are numerous. It is worth thinking about them in the light of the experience of earlier American immigrant groups.

Now I come to my last point. The most distinctive structural feature which may affect the acculturation and assimilation of Mexican-Americans in comparison with immigrant and ethnic groups of the great European immigration is the revolutionary change in the law and its constitutional interpretation of the 1960s and '70s designed to eliminate discrimination on the grounds of race and ethnic origin. Such change limits the actions, public and private, that may be taken to encourage or force acculturation and assimilation or to penalize those who do not change language, customs, loyalty and identity.

Now I want to make clear my point. I'm not saying that I prefer the forceful Americanization that took place in the '20s, the '30s or the '40s, or the degree of imposition of a national law which made it, for example, almost impossible for the American Jewish community in the 1940s to fight for more immigration of Jewish refugees. I'm not saying that was great and what we have now is bad. I'm saying that was different and what we now have is different. We have a different situation in law and sentiment, and in constitutional interpretation, which makes the forceful assimilation and acculturation of the past something of the past. If it happens, it will happen for other reasons. In other words, I will say these changes limit the actions, public and private, that may be taken to encourage or force accultura-tion and assimilation, or to penalize those who do not change language, customs, loyalty and identity.

National legislation, principally the Civil Rights Act of '64 and its expansion in '72, the Voting Rights Act of '65 and its expansions and renewals of '75 and '83, has created a radically new situation in this country compared to the period of the last mass immigration. Most important for the economic future of immigrant and ethnic groups is the prohibition of discrimina-tion in education and employment. Most important for their political future is the protection of political rights of persons who do not speak English, and the elimination of all tests and devices, in the language of the Voting Rights Act, including literacy tests, that may be used to prevent registering and voting. These acts are supplemented by regulations and legal interpretations and accompanied by an executive order requir-ing affirmative action in recruitment, employment, and promo-tion by government contractors. Major regulatory agencies— the Equal Employment Opportunity Commission, subdivisions of the Department of Justice, the Office of Federal Contract Compliance Programs—none of which existed 20 years ago— are engaged in the enforcement of these acts and orders. Major changes in the means of operation of employers, public and private, have resulted from these laws.

It is true that there is continual debate over the degree to which these laws and regulations are enforced, or should be enforced, and the extensiveness of the changes they have brought about. Undoubtedly, they were more strongly enforced under the administration of President Carter than they are under the administration of President Reagan. It is, neverthe-less, worthy of note that, despite changes of attitude and en-forcement strategy from administration to administration, the hard skeleton of law persists, and the scarcely less hard armature of regulation and executive order also persists unchanged after three and one-half years of Republican administration. Not a single change has been made in the laws, or in the regulations that have been adopted to enforce them. Indeed, the only changes in law that have occurred have been to strengthen these laws, as in the renewal of the Voting Rights Act in 1983. And the only potential legislation will also serve to strengthen these laws, in part because of the Reagan Administration's efforts to soften their legal interpretation in the courts.

From the point of view of the future of Mexican-American groups, the key import of these major legal changes of the 1960s and subsequent decades, and the way they have been enforced by federal agencies in courts, has been to place a legal brake on efforts to encourage a more rapid acquisition of English and a more rapid shedding of immigrant identity. One can speak Spanish and participate fully, at least as a voter in the political process. No test or device, such as the requirement to speak English, can be used to limit voting. Indeed, the anomaly of the present situation is that knowledge of English is still required to become a citizen but is not required to exercise political rights as a citizen. This complex of law also, to some extent, encourages maintenance of distinctive ethnic identity. It may make an employee of Hispanic background more attractive for employment or promotion as a means of enabling an employer to fulfill affirmative action requirements. Similarly, applicants to selective educational programs of Hispanic background may be benefited for that reason alone.

Now, obviously, the changes that have lessened pressures to acculturate and assimilate are not simply changes in law. They themselves reflect changes in popular attitudes. While major change has been a desire to eliminate discriminational grounds of race and ethnic origin, an enormous change in popular attitudes has also taken place concerning the legitimacy and desirability of imposing a common identity forcefully on immigrants and members of minority groups. The change has occurred in these groups, too. Most have embraced Americanization and shed old identities of their own volition in the past. The advocates of group maintenance and language maintenance in the old European groups were all from minorities with little weight in their own communities. They have now, in part because of changes that have taken place in American as a receiving society, a far greater weight.

This last feature of structural change leaves us in the same ambiguous position as do features discussed earlier. The structural change is real. Up to now, its consequences were to inhibit the powerful forces that acculturate and assimilate immigrants in the United States, and that, again and again, have prevented them from becoming nations within nations, and have prevented the United States from becoming—despite certain slogans—a nation of nations.

Whatever the changes in law and attitudes, and they are substantial indeed, other forces in American society seem to maintain their strength. One such force is simply American popular culture, once expressed primarily through the press and movies, and now through television. One is aware that there is a strong minority presence in the mass media, and that even television, expensive as it is, provides stations in Spanish beamed to the growing Mexican-American population. I suspect (I wish I knew) their content is what it was when the foreign-language press was the chief means of communication within American communities in the first three decades of this century. That is, I suspect even Spanish-language stations are still involved in education and Americanization, modulated by the specific needs and characteristics of the group. I may be wrong, but I would be surprised if the Spanish-language TV stations paid more attention to what is happening in Mexico than in San Antonio and Los Angeles, or more attention to a Mexican election than to an American one.

The second major force that I think is still operating is American politics. No immigrant or minority group in this country, regardless of size or weight, in any city or state, has ever found it to its advantage, or profit, to operate outside the two-party system. Operating within it brings powerful assimilating forces into play, even while one is engaged in the very process of advancing the interests of one's group. One sees these forces at work as Mexican-Americans who represent Mexican-American districts try to formulate a position on immigration. Their position seems to represent the interests of their constituency getting ahead in America much more than it does any interest, concrete or ideological, which competes with what we may conceive of as an American national interest.

A third powerful assimilative force of the past is, I believe, considerably weaker. That is the American public school. It has lost a good deal of its self-confidence as judges and minority advocates have been able, again and again, to overrule school administrators, local elected leaders, and public opinion in the search for desegregation. It has lost more self-confidence as civil libertarians have limited the disciplinary powers of teachers, principals and administrators. It has had imposed on it complex and ambiguous requirements for bilingual education, and it has been buffeted by demands for recognition of the culture of the new immigrants. Little enough of all this has been done, complain the advocates of all these changes. They may have a point, but if little has been done positively, enough has been done negatively to undermine the sense of the public schools that they have a mission to reshape children of different cultures and languages into a common format—a conviction which dominated the public schools, I would say, until twenty years ago.

To tote up the balance with any confidence is premature. The Mexican-American immigration still flows heavily; our guess is it will flow more heavily in the future. I think we are more or less in the position we would be in 1910 in trying to figure how the massive flow of immigrants from Eastern Europe and Italy would work out in American society. Any effort to discern the future may be as badly off as a similar effort would have been then. Nevertheless, the structural features that may make a difference to Mexican-Americans are, I believe, real, and not insignificant. Up until now, their effect seems to fade before the powerful assimilatory forces—cultural, economic, and political—in American life. That is the way I believe most Americans would want it. It may be the way most Mexican-Americans would want it, too, but as long as these distinctive structural features are evident, there will always be a considerable uneasiness in elite and mass public opinion in the United States in observing the course of Mexican-American development.

Question:

I'm interested in your fifth structural factor, about the demise of assimilation. That's only true for Mexican-Americans. I work with Southeast Asian refugees. I consistently see legislation proposed to pass regulations to force Southeast Asians to assimilate as quickly as possible. All legislation has the goal of economic and social self-sufficiency. There is an 18-month to 36-month cutoff with regulations about entering into the United States and with regard to nuclear families as opposed to extended families. We want people to fit the American model family. There was legislation proposed just last week in the state of California to require Southeast Asians to learn the "Western work ethic." Refugees are now required to spend a longer time in transient centers to learn English, and to go through a very vigorous acculturation/orientation program. Clearly it is the attempt of the American government to make sure that these particular ethnic groups assimilate as quickly as possible. I'm wondering whether or not that is a re-emergence of attitude towards forced assimilation for certain groups?

Glazer:

Well, your comment is extremely interesting, and I think there's a special reason for that, which probably doesn't apply to the Mexican-Americans. The special reason is that they come in under refugee status. Refugee status gives you a lot of control.

It means if you don't do this, we won't let you in. It means you have to give a special definition of what is a refugee, and there is also an international arrangement for different countries to take them and the countries apply their own standards. I assume the French, who have done a really remarkable job in taking a lot of the Vietnamese, apply the standard that they ought to know French, which, if they came from the French educational system, they do. So the paradox is, the fact that we help them means that we can control them more. The fact that we give them special benefits, which Mexican-Americans don't have, (and Blacks have complained in Miami that Cubans have them while the Blacks don't, all of which is true), also means that we can legislate the notion that they ought to become Americans and be Americans.

Now, with the Mexican-Americans, first of all they come in under legal immigrant status or with a Green Card, which only involves the fact that you don't become a public charge. It doesn't involve any commitments on learning English, or the Western work ethic, or anything else. Secondly, a lot of it comes in not under control at all. So I think there is a somewhat different situation there. I think there's also structurally a different situation. The Asian groups are small, relatively speaking. There were fourteen million, in the last census, who identified themselves as Hispanic-Americans, the majority of whom are Mexican-Americans. In case of Asian groups, even the older ones do not even reach a million. So I think that for these groups, there would be a very much stronger assimilatory pressure from American society. I think a large group has a different history, course, and so on, than a small group. The point you raise is interesting, and I suppose its main import will be, will we see legislation like that affecting Hispanic-Americans?

Question:

You mentioned that Mexico's proximity to the United States sets it apart from previous migrations to the United States. I wonder if, as an element of that, you would address the question of what I call the "shuttle back and forth"—the fact that so many of them are likely to return to their village of origin may lessen their desire to learn English. Will proximity work against this particular group's learning English very quickly?

Glazer:

Well, I think that's certainly an implication of the adjacency. Another case is that of Puerto Ricans in New York. There you have the additional factor that their legal political status doesn't change if they go back and forth, and the flows are very much dependent on economic circumstances. In 1961, when I was studying Puerto Ricans in New York, I expected them to do much better than they did economically, and for various reasons I was just wrong. I wonder to what extent the fact that this is not a cut-off group, wasn't like other immigrant groups that just came to stay was a factor. You know there have been very big returns to Italy and to Greece, and so on, but still it can't be the same as going back to Puerto Rico in terms of cost, in terms of political control, in terms of implications. I think Mexican-Americans are somewhat in that position. Assimilation, whatever that means, or adaptation to a new country, depends so much on expectation, on what attitude you come with. That has always been very complicated. I would suspect one of the reasons Jews are as successful as they are is because they knew there was no place to go back to. I would suspect Armenians are as successful as they are—it's a small group—for the same reason: no place to go back to. There is no Armenia any more. There is Soviet Armenia if you went back, but there is that factor saying we're here, this is it, and we'll have to make the best of it.

Now that obviously creates a great incentive to relate yourself as best as possible to the new society. If the orientation is as it was for some of the Italian immigrants who were here to work for the construction season and to go back, then, as we know from the old statistics, and very few became citizens, and very few learned English. They developed a kind of antagonism to the American public school, and there is no question that this hampered their assimilation and acculturation.

Question:

There are two things I would like your opinion about. One is the perception that seems to exist among some people that bilingual education has run its course and is no longer seen to be very effective. The other is that we face some very difficult situations regarding the political implications of the state of California requiring prospective teachers to take proficiency tests, including English proficiency tests, before they can get a teaching credential. Many Mexican-American students see this as "fishy" and say, "I won't pass the test, I won't bother."

Glazer:

Well, you've raised a very important practical question. On bilingual education, I've written various things and my position now is as follows: I think that one has to make use of the native language in teaching. I take a pragmatic attitude towards it. Let me say two things. The major objective has to be English. I don't think, realistically, this can become the kind of bilingual society or trilingual society that Switzerland is, or some other countries are, with an equal level of development—one section talks Spanish, another section talks English. Miami comes close but it's not going to happen. It is a national society, so English is crucially important. The issue then becomes the role of Spanish from this pragmatic point of view (or the role of any other foreign language). I think, ideally, one emphasizes very strongly the acquisition of English, but one needs a lot of Spanish-speaking personnel in the schools. Now, I don't mean teachers who can pass a Spanish test and can't speak Spanish. I mean Spanish-speaking personnel. These could be of the order of teacher's aides, or you can give them another title, translators or something. I think that the people who have the interest of the children at heart, and, assuming that they see them as permanent residents of the United States, push for whatever measures lead to a rapid acquisition of English, will do them most good.

I think that there are other things we have learned from the past. We don't want to wipe out Spanish; it's a very important language, and there has to be a mechanism to maintain it, which means teaching in Spanish, too. But the teaching in Spanish must be clearly identified as something which is an advantage the child has which must not be lost, and therefore we will teach you Spanish language, grammar, literature, and so forth. That would have to be a very different kind of bilingual school system than what we've had. In other words, I'm proposing as a kind of ideal, something like Jewish day schools which are run half in Hebrew and half in English, where it's perfectly clear that our job is teaching English and teaching subjects in English, but, since there is a certain advantage, we'll teach part of the day in Spanish. That has to be done at a high level and can't be done as a means either to employ a lot of teachers, or to make people happy because Spanish is in the schools.

The specific problem you describe is a serious one, and one of the ways I would consider it is to say, "Are these tests unfairly penalizing?" If the tests have that kind of problem they ought to be fought.

Question:

If you are writing a paper comparing the integration and assimilation of Hispanic groups with previous groups and you talk about these five structural variables, but you don't deal with the number of illegal immigrants, you have left something out. Secondly, I would like to ask you about the correct laws regarding political refugees. How do we decide who is to be let in.

Glazer:

Well, on your first point, I will certainly take it to heart and you are right. I mean, there was no easy way of being an illegal immigrant before 1924.... The only ones who didn't get in had tuberculosis or something. Now, the fact that a large percentage of the community lives under the pressures and realities of illegality must be an enormous influence with consequences I can't figure out, and your point is very well taken and I'll give you credit if I put it into the paper. Illegal status is a major structural variable—I think it is. On the second point, we did pass a law (and here I can't reconstruct the whole situation) on political refugee status, and there is a way of coming in as a refugee. The enforcement of the law or the administration of the law is subject, as you know, to tremendous political pressures in which it is up to the State Department to decide whether you're a refugee or not, and basically our history has been such that we accept refugees from Communist states and we find it very hard to allow refugee status to those from others, particularly if we are supporting their government. So we have the situation of Haitians, the situation of Salvadoreans, many of whom are claiming refugee status which in most cases is not being allowed by the State Department. We may criticize the American position. I haven't really studied it closely. My journal (*Public Interest*) will be publishing an article on the refugee problem, the refugee bill, and who gets refugee status. Let me point out that this is a problem other countries are facing, too. Turks in Germany, many of whom are illegal, have overwhelmed the German government by claims of refugee status, as have Iranians, who may have a stronger claim. Therefore, laws that were passed on the assumption that we deal with either small numbers of people who are political leaders and are in danger, or a kind of political expulsion, such as in Cuba, are now being overwhelmed by a kind of immigration which has a mix of economic and political features. We now have the kind of immigrant who does not fall under refugee status as the law was envisaged—you know, with a country like Haiti, anyone can legitimately consider himself a political refugee, I suppose. I think it's just one of those dilem-

42

mas in immigration policy and law which we have not yet been able to sort out.

Question:

There is an article I think you should read, published in 1973 in the Futurist. It's a kind of wild and woolly approach to the potentiality of Hispanic or Mexican and other Latin American immigration to the United States as "a population time-bomb." They have marvelous scenarios in which they press everything way beyond logic, including the adoption of Spanish as the legal language of the United States. I agree with a great deal of what you've said, but I think you've missed a couple of very important points. First of all, I think if you will read the statistics on what's happening in cities along the border, and throughout the border region—never mind about the obvious ones that you can't help seeing like San Diego—if you'll start with Brownsville-Matamoros, go all the way down to El Paso-Juarez, you'll find you have a whole region in which the smallest proportion of Hispanic-identity citizens is 60 percent going on 80 percent, and where the larger ones are 80 percent going on 95 percent. The notion that somehow this is going to become an Anglo society which still remembers when they once spoke Spanish, I am going to submit, is really a misreading of reality altogether. There is no issue of bilingual education, because the question is, are you going to speak English as well as Spanish, not are you going to speak Spanish as well as English. I am not talking about it as a device for assimilating into the United States. You have ethnic cities now where you don't just have dominance, you have predominance, and where the language of the marketplace, of the people is already Spanish and will remain so—it will not change. I think you are absolutely wrong and do not understand what is going on. I realize there's a lot of curvature of the earth between Boston and New York and the border of Texas and Arizona and New Mexico, but if you look over it, you'll see things that have never happened before. I think that another part of that is very important for you to keep in mind is that the orientation of Hispanics is really, so far as I can tell, a petty bourgeois orientation. You're dealing with a kind of third world capitalism, you're dealing with a kinship capitalism and that kind of shop keeping and peculiarly what was necessary to become rapidly successful immigrants in 1910. Finally, I don't think you've taken account of another very major structural change, and that is if you look at where the Anglos live in great metropolitan centers, you're no longer looking at something that can be called suburbia. You're looking at an external outer metropolis, not organized as a single government, but with a sense of cultural class homogeneity. These are two quite separate societies and the struggles between them are also going to be struggles between inner cities where Hispanic peoples have to become dominant, if not also predominant, and outer metropolises populated primarily by Anglos. That's the kind of political problem we've never had before. And we can assume, I think, that some of the models you're talking about are genuinely archaic.

Glazer:

Well, those are very interesting comments. I'm sure I could learn a lot more if we kept on going, as I already feel I have. We'll have to continue this in other settings, and I appreciate all the comments on what was admittedly a look from a distant perspective.

3

BIBLIOGRAPHY

The bibliography that follows has been compiled by means of a systematic search of a wide variety of bibliographic indices which cover the years 1945 through 1985. It is arranged in two large categories: work by Glazer and work about topics related to this lecture.

By Glazer

Books

Affirmative Discrimination: Ethnic Inequality and Public Policy. New York: Basic Books, 1975.

American Judaism. 2nd ed. Chicago: University of Chicago Press, 1957.

With Daniel P. Moynihan. *Beyond the Melting Pot: The Negroes, Puerto-Ricans, Jews, Italians, and Irish of New York City.* 2d ed. Cambridge, Mass.: M.I.T. Press, 1963.

Cities in Trouble. Chicago: Quadrangle Books, 1970.

Clamor at the Gates: The New American Immigration. San Francisco: ICS Press, 1985.

Ethnic Dilemmas, 1964-1982. Cambridge, Mass.: Harvard University Press, 1983.

Ethnic Pluralism and Public Policy: Achieving Equality in the U.S. and Britain. Lexington, Mass.: Lexington Books, 1983.

Ethnicity: Theory and Experience. Cambridge, Mass.: Harvard University Press, 1975.

The Public Interest on Crime and Punishment. Cambridge, Mass.: Abt Books, 1984.

Remembering the Answers: Essays on the American Student Revolt. New York: Basic Books, 1970.

The Social Basis of American Communism. New York: Harcourt, Brace, 1961.

Articles

"The 'Alienation' of Modern Man." *Commentary,* April 1947, 378-385.

"America's Ethnic Pattern." *Commentary,* April 1953, 401-408.

"The American People and Cold War Policy." *Commentary,* May 1954, 461-465.

"'The American Soldier' As Science." *Commentary,* November 1949, 487-496.

"American Values and American Foreign Policy." *Commentary,* July 1976, 32-37.

"An Answer to Lillian Hellman." *Commentary*, June 1976, 36-39.

"The Attack on the Professions." *Commentary*, November 1978, 34-41.

"The Authoritarian Personality in Profile." *Commentary*, June 1950, 573-583.

With Philip Selznick. "Berkeley." *Commentary*, March 1965, 80-85.

"Black English and Reluctant Judges." *Public Interest* 62 (Winter 1981): 40-54.

"Black and Ethnic Groups: The Difference and the Political Difference It Makes." *Social Problems* 18 (Spring 1971): 444-461.

"Blacks, Jews and the Intellectuals." *Commentary*, April 1969, 33-39.

"Blood." *Public Interest* 24 (Summer 1971): 86-94.

"A Breakdown in Civil Rights Enforcement?" *Public Interest* 23 (Spring 1971): 106-115.

"Capitalism, Socialism and Democracy." A Symposium. *Commentary*, April 1978, 45-46.

"City Problems and Jewish Responsibilities." *Commentary*, January 1962, 24-30.

"Cuba and the Peace Movement." *Commentary*, December 1962, 514-518.

"Ethnic Groups and Education: Towards the Tolerance of Difference." *Journal of Negro Education* 38 (Summer 1969): 187-195.

"Ethnic Groups in America: From National Culture to Ideology." In *Freedom and Control in Modern Society*, edited by Morroe

Bergerm, Theodore Abel and Charles H. Page. New York: D. Van Nostrand Co., 1954.

"Ethnicity—North, South, West." *Commentary*, May 1982, 73-78.

"Ethnicity and the Schools." *Commentary*, September 1974, 55-59.

"The Exposed American Jew." *Commentary*, June 1975, 25-30.

"Four Rabbis in Search of Judaism." *Commentary*, February 1955, 151-154.

"Freedom and Ethnicity: The Experiences of the United States." *Publius* 7 (1977): 11-88.

"The Future of the Welfare State: II. Towards a Self-Service Society?" *Public Interest* 70 (Winter 1983): 66-90.

"The Future of the Welfare State: IV. The Social Policy of the Reagan Administration: A Review." *Public Interest* 75 (Spring 1984): 76-98.

"The Good Society." *Commentary*, September 1963, 226-234.

"Government by Manipulation." *Commentary*, July 1946, 81-86.

"Hannah Arendt's America." *Commentary*, September 1975, 61-67.

"Herbert H. Lehman of New York." *Commentary*, May 1963, 403-409.

"Housing Problems and Housing Policies." *Public Interest* 7 (Spring 1967): 21-51.

"How Has the United States Met Its Major Challenges Since 1945?" A Symposium. *Commentary*, November 1985, 41-44.

"Human Rights and American Foreign Policy." A Symposium. *Commentary*, November 1981, 36-38.

"The Immigrant Groups in American Culture." *Yale Review* 68 (Spring 1959): 382-387.

"The Integration of American Immigrants." *Law and Contemporary Problems* 21 (Spring 1956): 256-259.

"Interests and Passions." *Public Interest* 81 (Fall 1985): 17-30.

"I.Q. on Trial." *Commentary*, June 1981, 51-59.

"Is Busing Necessary?" *Commentary*, March 1972, 39-52.

"Is 'Integration' Possible in New York Schools?" *Commentary*, September 1960, 185-193.

"Is New York Ungovernable?" *Commentary*, September 1961, 185-193.

"The Jewish Revival in America: II." *Commentary*, January 1956, 17-24.

"Liberalism and the Jews." *Commentary*, January 1980, 37-38.

"Liberalism and the Negro: A Round-Table Discussion." *Commentary*, March 1964, 25-42.

"The Limits of Social Policy." *Commentary*, September 1971, 51-58.

With Milton Himmelfare. "McGovern and the Jews." *Commentary*, September 1972, 43-51.

"The Method of Senator McCarthy." *Commentary*, March 1953, 244-256.

"More Insanity Than a Century Ago?" *Commentary*, December 1953, 587-589.

"The Negro American." *Public Interest* 3 (Spring 1966): 108-115.

"Negroes and Jews: A New Challenge to Pluralism." *Commentary*, December 1964, 29-34.

"The New Left and Its Limits." *Commentary*, July 1968 31-39.

"New Light on 'The Authoritarian Personality.'" *Commentary*, March 1954, 289-297.

"A New Look at the Melting Pot." *Commentary* 16 (Summer 1969): 180-187.

"New York's Puerto Ricans." *Commentary*, December 1958, 469-478.

"Nixon, the Great Society, and the Future of Social Policy." A Symposium. *Commentary*, May 1973, 34-39.

"Notes on Southern California." *Commentary*, August 1959, 100-107.

"On Being Deradicalized." *Commentary*, October 1970, 74-80.

"On Jewish Forebodings." *Commentary*, August 1985, 32-36.

"On Subway Graffiti in New York." *Public Interest* 54 (Winter 1979): 3-11.

"Paradoxes of American Poverty." *Public Interest* 1 (Fall 1965): 76-81.

"Paradoxes of Health Care." *Public Interest* 22 (Winter 1971): 62-77.

"Paris—The View From New York." *Public Interest* 74 (Winter 1984): 31-51.

"The Parlor Terrorists." *Commentary*, January 1947, 55-58.

"The Peace Movement in America . . . 1961." *Commentary*, April 1961, 288-296.

"Perspectives on Health Care." *Public Interest* 31 (Spring 1973): 110-125.

"Political Mobilization: Mexican Americans in Comparative Perspective." Paper presented at the conference on "Lessons From Other Societies: Mexican Americans in Comparative Perspective," sponsored by the Urban Institute, Los Angeles, Calif., March 1984.

"Poverty, Welfare, and Income Maintenance. II. Beyond Income Maintenance—A Note on Welfare in New York City." *Public Interest* 16 (Summer 1969): 102-122.

"The Puerto-Ricans." *Commentary*, July 1963, 1-9.

"The Rediscovery of the Family." *Commentary*, March 1978, 49-56.

"Reform Work, Not Welfare." *Public Interest* 40 (Summer 1975): 3-10.

"Regulating Business and the Universities: One Problem or Two?" *Public Interest* 56 (Summer 1979): 43-65.

"The Role of the Intellectual." *Commentary*, February 1971, 55-61.

"Rumblings on the Pastorals Left." *Commentary*, December 1948, 563-565.

"Should Judges Administer Social Services?" *Public Interest* 50 (Winter 1978): 64-80.

"Social Science and the Arts. Christo in Central Park—and in Harlem." *Public Interest* 68 (Summer 1982): 70-77.

"Strategies for Integration: On 'Opening up' the Suburbs." *Public Interest* 37 (Fall 1974): 89-111.

"The Street Gangs and Ethnic Enterprise." *Public Interest* 28 (Summer 1972): 82-89.

"'Student Power' in Berkeley." *Public Interest* 13 (Fall 1968): 3-21.

"The Study of Man." *Commentary*, November 1945, 84-87.

"Toward an Imperial Judiciary?" *Public Interest* 41 (Fall 1975): 104-123.

"Vietnam: The Case for Immediate Withdrawal." *Commentary*, May 1971, 33-37.

"What Americans Get Out of College." *Commentary*, May 1952, 486-490.

"What Happened at Berkeley." *Commentary*, February 1965, 39-47.

"What Is Sociology's Job?" *Commentary*, February 1947, 181-186.

"What Opinion Polls Can and Can't Do." *Commentary*, August 1951, 181-184.

"What Sociology Knows About American Jews." *Commentary*, March 1950, 275-284.

"Who Wants Higher Education, Even When It's Free?" *Public Interest* 39 (Spring 1975): 130-135.

"Why Bakke Won't End Reverse Discrimination." *Commentary*, September 1978, 36-41.

With Daniel P. Moynihan. "Why Ethnicity?" *Commentary*, October 1974, 33-39.

"Why Jews Stay Sober." *Commentary*, February 1952, 181-186.

U.S. Immigration Policy

Books

American Council for Nationalities Service. *The Immigration Acts of October 3, 1965 and April 7, 1970.* New York: American Council for Nationalities Service, 1965.

Bennett, Marion T. *American Immigration Policies: A History.* Washington, D.C.: Public Affairs Press, 1963.

Briggs, Vernon M., Jr. *Foreign Labor Programs as an Alternative to Illegal Immigration into the United States: A Dissenting View.* College Park, Md.: Center For Philosophy and Public Policy, University of Maryland, 1980.

————. *Immigration Policy and the American Labor Force.* Baltimore, Md.: Johns Hopkins University Press, 1984.

Bustamante, Jorge A. *U.S. Immigration Policy: A Mexican Perspective on President Reagan's Proposal.* Washington, D.C.: Overseas Council, 1982.

Calavita, Kitty. *California's "Employer Sanctions": The Case of the Disappearing Law.* La Jolla, Calif.: Center For U.S.-Mexican Studies, University of California, San Diego, 1982.

Chandrasekhar, S., ed. *From India to America: A Brief History of Immigration, Problems of Discrimination, Admission and Assimilation.* La Jolla, Calif.: Population Review Publications, 1982.

Chiswick, Barry R. *The Gateway: U.S. Immigration Issues and Policies.* Washington, D.C.: American Enterprise Institute for Public Policy Research, 1982.

————. "Guidelines for the Reform of Immigration Policy." In *Essays in Contemporary Economic Problems, 1981/1982*, edited by William Fellner. Washington, D.C.: American Enterprise Institute, 1981.

Christol, Helen and Serge Ricard, eds. *Hyphenated Diplomacy: European Immigration and U.S. Foreign Policy, 1914-1984*. Aix-en-Provence: Groupe de Recherche et d'Etudes Nord Américaines, for the European Association for American Studies, 1985.

Congressional Research Service. *U.S. Immigration Law and Policy: 1952-1979*. Washington, D.C.: Library of Congress, 1979.

Copp, Nelson Gage. "'Wetbacks' and Braceros: Mexican Migrant Laborers and American Immigration Policy, 1930-1960." Ph.D. dissertation, Boston University, 1963.

Cornelius, Wayne A. *Mexican Migration to the U.S.: The Limits of Government Intervention*. La Jolla, Calif.: Program in U.S.-Mexican Studies, University of California, San Diego, 1981.

————. *Legalizing the Flow of Temporary Migrant Workers From Mexico: A Policy Proposal*. La Jolla, Calif.: Program in U.S.-Mexican Studies, University of California, San Diego, 1981.

Cornelius, Wayne A. and Ricardo A. Montoya. eds. *America's New Immigration Law: Origins, Rationales and Potential Consequences*. La Jolla, Calif.: Center for U.S.-Mexican Studies, University of California, San Diego, 1983.

————. eds. *The Report of the U.S. Select Commission on Immigration and Refugee Policy: A Critical Analysis*. La Jolla, Calif.: Center for U.S.-Mexican Studies, University of California, San Diego, 1983.

Dimas, Nicasio. *The Tarnished Golden Door: Civil Rights Issues in Immigration*. U.S. Commission on Civil Rights, GPO, 1980.

Harper, Elizabeth J. *Immigration Laws of the United States.* 3rd ed. Indianapolis: Bobbs-Merrill Co., 1975.

Handlin, Oscar. *Hearings Before the President's Commission on Immigration and Naturalization.* 82nd Cong., 2nd sess, Washington, D.C.: GPO, 1952.

Hofstetter, Richard R., ed. *U.S. Immigration Policy.* Durham, N.C.: Duke University Press, 1984.

Hutchinson, E.P. *Legislative History of American Immigration Policy, 1798-1965.* Philadelphia: University of Pennsylvania Press, 1981.

In Defense of the Alien. Immigration and Refugee Policy. New York: Proceedings of the 1983 Annual National Legal Conference on Immigration and Refugee Policy, April 21 and 22, 1983.

Joint Hearings Before the Subcommittee on Immigration and Refugee Policy of the Senate Committee on the Judiciary and Subcommittee on Immigration, Refugees, and International Law of the House Committee on the Judiciary. 96th Cong., 1st sess., 7 May 1981, Washington, D.C.: GPO, 1981.

Library of Congress. *Congressional Research Service. U.S. Immigration Law and Policy 1952-79.* Washington, D.C.: U.S. GPO, 1979.

North, David S. "Enforcing the Immigration Law: A Review of the Options." In *U.S. Immigration Policy and the National Interest,* Appendix E, papers on Illegal Aliens, Select Commission on Immigration and Refugee Policy, Washington, D.C.: 1981.

North, David S. and Jennifer R. Wagner. "Enforcing the Immigration Law: A Review of the Options." Prepared for Select Commission on Immigration and Refugee Policy, Washington, D.C.: June 1980.

Papademtrion, Demetrios G. and Mark J. Miller. eds. *The Unavoidable Issue: U.S. Immigration Policy in the 1980s.* Philadelphia: Institute For the Study of Human Issues, 1983.

Tanton, John. "Rethinking Immigration Policy," in *Immigration Papers I.* USA: Federation for American Immigration Reform, January 1979.

U.S. Select Commission on Immigration and Refugee Policy. *U.S. Immigration Policy and the National Interest.* Final Report and Recommendations of the Select Commission on Immigration and Refugee Policy to the Congress and the President of the United States, 1 March 1981.

———. *U.S. Immigration Policy and the National Interest: Staff Report.* Washington, D.C.: G.P.O., 1981.

United States. Congress. House. *Amending the Immigration and Nationality Act and For Other Purposes* 89th Cong., 1st sess., 6 August 1965, H. Rept. 745.

———. ———. Senate. *Amending the Immigration and Nationality Act and For Other Purposes.* 89th Cong., 1st sess., 15 September 1965, S. Rept. 748.

———. ———. ———. Committee on the Judiciary. *U.S. Immigration Law and Policy, 1952-1979.* Washington, D.C.: GPO, 1979.

U.S. Department of Justice. *U.S. Immigration and Refugee Policy.* Washington, 30 July 1981.

U.S. Departments of Justice, Labor and State. *Interagency Task Force on Immigration Policy,* a staff report. G.P.O., August 1979.

Vialet, Joyce, ed. *Selected Readings on U.S. Immigration Policy and Law.* Washington, D.C.: Library of Congress, Congressional Research Service, 1980.

————. *U.S. Immigration Policy: The Western Hemisphere*. Washington: Library of Congress, Congressional Research Service, 9 April 1980.

Zolberg, Aristide. "The Main Gate and the Back Door: The Politics of American Immigration Policy, 1950-1976." Paper Delivered at the Council on Foreign Relations, Washington, D.C., April 1978.

Articles

Abrams, Elliot and Franklin S. Abrams. "Immigration Policy: Who Gets In and Why?" *The Public Interest* 38(1975): 3-29.

Bernard, William S. "America's Immigration Policy: Its Evolution and Sociology." *International Migration Review* 2 No. 4 (1965).

"Bill on Immigration: Diversity in House's Debate." *New York Times* 17 June 1984.

Cardenas, Gilbert. "United States Immigration Policy Toward Mexico: A Historical Perspective." *Chicano Law Review*, 2 (Summer 1975).

Cornelius, Wayne A. "Undocumented Immigration: A Critique of the Carter Administration's Policy Proposals." *Migration Today* October 1977.

Fallows, James. "Immigrant Bill: A Blow." *New York Times* 9 October 1983.

Flores, Estevan T. "1982 Simpson-Mazzoli Immigration Reform and the Hispanic Community." *La Red/The Net* (Newsletter of the National Chicano Council on Higher Education), February 1983, 14-16.

Fragomen, Austin T., Jr. "Immigration and Nationality Act Amendments of 1981." *International Migration Review* 16, No. 1 (Spring 1982): 206-222.

Greene, Sheldon L. "Public Agency Distortion of Congressional Will: Federal Policy Toward Non-Resident Alien Labor." *George Washington Law Review* 40(March 1972).

Harwood, Edwin. "The Crisis in Immigration Policy." *Journal of Contemporary Studies* VI(Fall 1983): 47-52.

————. "Can Immigration Laws Be Enforced?" *Public Interest* 72(Summer 1983): 107-123.

"The Immigration Bills: A Comparison." *New York Times* 21 June 1984.

Kennedy, Edward M. "The Immigration Act of 1965." *Annals of the American Academy of Political and Social Sciences* 367(September 1966): 137-149.

————. "Refugee Act of 1980." *International Migration Review* 15(Spring 1981): 141-156.

McLennan, Kenneth and Malcolm Lovell, Jr. "Immigration Reform: An Economic Necessity." *Journal of the Institute for Socioeconomic Studies* 6(Summer 1981): 38-52.

Pear, Robert. "Aliens Bill Nears Reality." *New York Times* 18 June 1984.

————. "Ambitious Immigration Bill Fails as Charges of Blame Are Traded." *New York Times* 12 October 1984.

————. "Bill on Aliens a Divisive Issue For Democrats." *New York Times* 22 April 1984.

————. "Conference on Immigration Bill Stalls." *New York Times* 26 September 1984.

————. "House Backs Plan Legalizing Aliens in U.S. Before 1982." *New York Times* 18 June 1984.

————. "House, By 216-211, Approves Aliens Bill After Retaining Amnesty Plan in Final Test." *New York Times* 21 June 1984.

————. "House to Debate Immigration Bill Despite Pleas of Hispanic Groups." *New York Times* 12 June 1984.

————. "The Immigration Bill's Melting Pot." *New York Times* 2 July 1984.

————. "Immigration Reform is Alive and Well." *New York Times* 22 May 1983.

————. "Reagan Aides Draft a Plan to Let Mexicans Work in U.S. as Guests." *New York Times* 11 May 1981.

————. "Senate Approves Immigration Bill with Hiring Curb." *New York Times* 19 May 1983.

————. "Senate Votes a Sweeping Revision of the Nation's Immigration Laws." *New York Times* 18 August 1982.

Rodino, Peter Jr. "New Immigration Law in Retrospect." *International Migration Review* 2 (Summer 1968): 56-61.

Schuck, Peter H. "The Transformation of Immigration Law." *Columbia Law Review* 84(January 1984). 1-90.

Schwartz, Abba P. "The Role of the State Department in the Administration and Enforcement of the New Immigration Law."

"Southeast Asian Refugees in the U.S.A.: Case Studies in Adjustment and Policy Implications." *Anthropological Quarterly* 55(July 1982).

Teitelbaum, Michael S. "Political Asylum in Theory and Practice." *The Public Interest* 76(Summer 1984): 74-86.

————. "Right Versus Right: Immigration and Refugee Policy in the Unites States." *Foreign Affairs* 59 (Fall 1980): 21-59.

"United States Policy on Mexican Immigration." *Current History* 80 (1981): 385.

Mexican Immigration

Books

Arias, Armando. "Undocumented Mexicans: A Study in the Social Psychology of Clandestine Migrations to the United States." Ph.D. dissertation, University of California, San Diego, 1981.

Arroyo, Luis Leobardo. *Prelude to the Future: Past and Present of Mexican Workers North of the Rio Bravo, 1600-1975.*

Ashabranner, Brent. *Dark Harvest: Migrant Farmworkers in America.* New York: Dodd, Mead and Co., 1985.

Bohning, W.R. *Studies in International Labor Migration.* New York: St. Martin's Press, 1984.

Borjas, George J., and Marta Tienda. *Hispanics in the U.S. Economy.* Orlando, Fla.: Academic Press Inc., 1985.

Briggs, Vernon M., Jr. *Mexican Migration and the U.S. Labor Market.* Austin: University of Texas Center for the Study of Human Resources and the Bureau of Business Research, Studies Human Resource Development, No. 3, 1975.

Bullock, Paul. "Employment Problems of the Mexican American." In

Mexican-Americans in the United States. Edited by John H. Burma. Cambridge: Schenkman, 1970.

Burma, John H. *Mexican-Americans in the U.S.* Canfield Press (Harper and Row) 1970.

Burrows, Edwin G. *Hawaiian Americans: An Account of the Mingling of Japanese, Chinese, Polynesian and American Culture.* New Haven: Yale University Press, 1947.

Bustamante, Jorge A. "Commodity-Migrants: Structural Analysis of Mexican Immigration to the United States." In *Views Across the Border: The United States and Mexico.* Edited by Stanley R. Ross. Albuquerque: University of New Mexico Press, 1978.

————. "Structural and Ideological Conditions of Undocumented Mexican Immigration to the U.S." In *Current Issues in Social Policy.* Edited by W. Boyd Lettrell and Gideon Sjoberg. Beverly Hills, Calif.: Sage Publications, 1976.

Cardenas, Gilberto. "Manpower Impact and Problems of Mexican Illegal Aliens in an Urban Labor Market." Ph.D. dissertation, University of Illinois, 1976.

Cardoso, Lawrence A. *Mexican Emigration to the United States 1897-1931.* Tucson: University of Arizona Press, 1980.

Cornelius, Wayne A. *Mexican Migration to the United States: The View from Rural Sending Communities.* Cambridge, Mass.: Migration and Development Study Group, MIT 1976.

————. *Mexican Migration to the United States: The States of Current Knowledge and Recommendations for Future Research.* La Jolla, Calif.: Center for United States-Mexican Studies, University of California, San Diego, 1979.

Cornelius, Wayne A., et al. *Mexican Immigrants in the San Francisco*

Bay Area: A Summary of Current Knowledge: A Report Prepared for the Bay Area and the World Project. La Jolla, Calif.: Center for United States-Mexican Studies, University of California, San Diego, 1982.

Cornelius, Wayne A.; Leo R. Chavez; and Jorge G. Castro. *Mexican Immigrants and Southern California: A Summary of Current Knowledge.* La Jolla, Calif.: Program in United States-Mexican Studies, University of California, San Diego, 1982.

Craig, Richard. *The Bracero Program: Interest Groups and Foreign Policy.* Austin: University of Texas Press, 1971.

Cross, Harry E. *Across the Border: Rural Development in Mexico and Recent Migration to the U.S.* Berkeley: Institute of Governmental Studies, University of California, Berkeley, 1981.

Davidson, John. *The Long Road North.* Garden City, N.J.: Doubleday, 1979.

Ehrlich, Paul R.; Loy Bilderback; and Anne Ehrlich. *The Golden Door: International Migration, Mexico and the United States.* New York and Toronto: Ballantine Books, 1978.

Fogel, Walter A. *Mexican Illegal Alien Workers in the United States.* Los Angeles: Institute of Industrial Relations, University of California, Los Angeles, 1978. (Monograph Series).

————. *United States Immigration Policy and Unsanctioned Migrants.* Los Angeles: Institute of Industrial Relations, University of California, Los Angeles, 1980.

————. *Mexican-Americans in Southwest Labor Markets.* Los Angeles: University of California Mexican-American Study Project, Advance Report 10, 1967.

Freeman, Gary P. *Immigrant Labor and Racial Conflict in Industrialized Societies.* Princeton: Princeton University Press, 1979.

Galarza, Ernesto. *Merchants of Labor: The Mexican Bracero Story.* Charlotte, N.C.: McNally and Loftin, 1964.

————. *Farm Workers and Agri-Business in California, 1947-1960.* Notre Dame: University of Notre Dame, 1977.

Gamio, Manuel. *The Mexican Immigrant.* New York: Arno Press, 1969.

————. *Mexican Immigration to the U.S.* Chicago: The University of Chicago Press, 1930.

Garcia y Griego, Manuel. *The Importation of Mexican Contract Laborers to the U.S., 1942-1964: Antecedents, Operation and Legacy.* La Jolla: Program in U.S.-Mexican Studies, University of California, San Diego, 1980.

De la Garza, Rodolfo O., and Robert R. Brichetto. *The Mexican American Electorate: Information Sources and Policy Orientations.* San Antonio: Southwest Voter Registration Education Project and the Center for Mexican American Studies, University of Texas at Austin, 1983.

Gonzales, Juan L., Jr. *Mexican-American Farm Workers: The California Agricultural Industry.* Praeger, 1985.

Grebler, Leo; Joan W. Moore; and Ralph C. Guzmann. *The Mexican-American People: The Nation's Second Largest Minority.* New York: The Free Press, 1970.

Haas, Lisbeth. *The Bracero in Orange County: A Work Force for Economic Transition.* La Jolla, Calif.: Program in U.S.-Mexican Studies, University of California, San Diego, 1981.

Jones, Richard C., ed. *Patterns of Undocumented Migration: Mexico and the United States.* Totowa, N.J.: Rowman and Allanheld, 1984.

————. *Undocumented Migration from Mexico: Some Geographical Questions.* San Antonio: Human Resources Management and Development Program, College of Business, University of Texas at San Antonio, 1981.

Kiser, George C., and Martha Woody Kiser, eds. *Mexican Workers in the U.S.: Historical and Political Perspectives.* Albuquerque: University of New Mexico Press, 1979.

Kirstein, Peter Neil. *Anglo Over Bracero: A History of the Mexican Worker in the U.S. From Roosevelt to Nixon.* San Francisco: R & E Research Associates, 1977.

Lesko Associates. *Final Report: Basic Data and Guidance Required to Implement a Major Illegal Alien Study,* prepared for the U.S. Immigration and Naturalization Service. Washington, D.C., 15 October 1975.

Lewis, Sasha Gregory. *Slave Trade Today: American Exploitation of Illegal Aliens.* Boston: Beacon Press, 1979.

Lipschultz, Robert J. "American Attitudes Toward Mexican Immigration, 1924-1952." Ph.D. dissertation, University of Chicago, 1962.

Maram, Sheldon L., with Stewart Long and Dennis Berg. *Hispanic Workers in the Garment and Restaurant Industries in Los Angeles County.* Fullerton: California State University Fullerton, 1980.

Martin, Philip L. and David S. North. "Nonimmigrant Aliens in American Agriculture." Paper delivered at the Conference on Seasonal Agricultural Labor Markets in the United States, Washington, D.C., 10 January 1980.

McWilliams, Carey. *North From Mexico: The Spanish-Speaking People of the United States*. New York: Greenwood, 1968.

————. *Factories in the Field: The Story of Migratory Farm Labor in California*. Boston: Little, Brown, 1939.

Meador, Bruce Staffel. *"Wetback" Labor in the Lower Rio Grande Valley*. San Francisco: R & E Research Associates, 1973.

Miller, Mark J. and David J. Yeres. "A Massive Temporary Worker Programme for the U.S.: Solution or Mirage?" Working paper for Migration for Employment Programme, International Labor Organization, Geneva, Switzerland, November 1979.

Mines, Richard. *Developing a Community Tradition of Migration to the U.S.: A Field Study in Rural Zacatecas, Mexico, and California Settlement Areas*. La Jolla, Calif: Program in U.S.-Mexican Studies, University of California, San Diego, 1981.

Moore, Joan W. *Mexican Americans*. Englewood Cliffs, N.J.: Prentice-Hall, 1976.

Musgrave, Peggy B., ed. *Mexico and the U.S.: Studies in Economic Interaction*. Boulder, Colo.: Westview, 1985.

Navlen, Joseph and Frederickson, Craig. *The Employer's View, Is There a Need for a Guestworker Program?* San Diego: Community Research Associates, 1982.

Newton, Horace Edwin. *Mexican Illegal Immigration into California, Principally Since 1945: A Socio-Economic Study*. San Francisco: R & E Research Associates, 1973.

North, David S. *Alien Workers: A Study of the Labor Certification Program*. Washington, D.C.: Transcentury Corp., 1971.

————. *The Border Crossers: People Who Live in Mexico and Work in the U.S.* Washington, D.C.: Transcentury Corp., 1970.

————. "Comments on Vernon Brigg's Paper." Paper Delivered at the Conference on Border Relations, La Paz, Mexico, 8 February 1980.

————. *Immigrants and the American Labor Market.* Washington, D.C.: Manpower Research Monograph, No.31, U.S. Dept. of Labor, 1974.

————. *Seven Years Later: The Experience of the 1970 Cohort of Immigrants in the U.S. Labor Market.* Washington, D.C.: Linton & Co., 1978.

North, David S., and Marion F. Houston. *The Characteristics and Role of Illegal Aliens in the U.S. Labor Market: An Exploratory Study.* Washington, D.C.: New Transcentury Foundation: Linton, 1976.

North, David S. and Allen LeBel. *Manpower and Immigration Policies in the United States.* Washington, D.C.: National Commission for Manpower Policy, 1978.

North, David S. and Jennifer R. Wagner. *Nonimmigrant Workers in the U.S.: Current Trends and Future Implications.* Washington, D.C.: Department of Labor, 1980.

————. *Government Records: What They Tell Us About the Role of Illegal Immigrants in the Labor Market and in Income Transfer Programs.* Washington, D.C.: New Transcentury Foundation, 1981.

North, David S. and William G. Weisart. *Immigrants and the American Labor Market.* Washington: Transcentury Corp, 1973.

Piore, Michael J. *Birds of Passage: Migrant Labor Industrial Societies.* Cambridge, New York: Cambridge University Press, 1979.

————. *Undocumented Workers and U.S. Immigration Policy.* Cambridge, Mass.: Migration and Development Study Group, Center for International Studies, Massachusetts Institute of Technology, 1977.

Portes, Alejandro. "Why Illegal Migration? A Structural Perspective." Latin American Immigration Project Occasional Papers, Department of Sociology, Duke University, Durham, North Carolina, November 1977.

Portes, Alejandro, and Robert L. Bach. *Latin Journey: Cuban and Mexican Immigrants in the United States.* Berkeley: University of California Press, 1985.

Portes, Alejandro and John Walton. *Labor, Class and the International System.* New York: Academic Press, 1981.

Power, Jonathan. *Migrant Workers in Western Europe and the United States.* In collaboration with Marguerite Garling and Anna Hardman. Oxford, N.Y.: Pergamon Press, 1979.

President's Commission on Migratory Labor. *Migratory Labor in American Agriculture: Report.* Washington, D.C.: GPO, 1951.

Labor Market Projections for the United States and Mexico and Their Relevance to Current Migration Controversies. Stanford, Calif.: Food Research Institute, Stanford University, 6 July 1978.

Roberts, Kenneth, et al. *The Mexican Number Game: An Analysis of the Lesko Estimate of the Undocumented Migration from Mexico to the United States.* Austin: Bureau of Business Research, University of Texas, 1978.

Runsted, David and Leveen, Phillip. *Mechanization and Mexican Labor in California Agriculture.* La Jolla, Calif.: Program in U.S.-Mexican Studies, University of California, San Diego, 1981.

San Diego County Border Task Force. *San Diego County Border Task Force Final Report, May 1980*, edited by John W. Pearson. San Diego: San Diego County Board of Supervisors, 1980.

Stoddard, Ellwyn R. "Selected Impacts of Mexican Migration on the U.S. Mexican Border." Paper presented to the State Department Select Panel on Border Problems, Washington, D.C., October 1978.

Stuart, James and Michael Kearney. *Causes and Effects of Agricultural Labor Migration from the Mixteca of Oaxaca to California*. La Jolla, Calif.: Program in U.S.-Mexican Studies, University of California, San Diego, 1981.

Sullivan, Teresa A. *Marginal Workers, Marginal Jobs: The Underutilization of American Workers*. Austin: University of Texas Press, 1978.

Taylor, Paul Schuster. *Mexican Labor in the United States*. New York: Arno Press, 1970.

Toney, William T. *A Descriptive Study of the Control of Illegal Mexican Migration in the Southwestern United States*. San Francisco: R & E Research Associates, 1977.

United States. Congress. House. Select Committee on Population. *Legal and Illegal Immigration to the United States*. Washington, D.C.: GPO, 1978.

————. ————. ————. Committee on International Relations, Subcommittee on the Inter-American Affairs. *Hearings, Undocumented Workers: Implications for United States Policy in the Western Hemisphere*. Washington, D.C.: GPO, 1978.

————. ————. Senate. Committee on the Judiciary. *Hearings, Caribbean Refugee Crisis: Cubans and Haitians*. Washington, D.C.: GPO, 1980.

————. ————. Committee on Labor and Public Welfare, Subcommittee on Migratory Labor. *Hearings on Migrant and Seasonal Farmworker Powerlessness.* 91st Cong., 1st and 2d sess., 21 May 1969.

————. Department of Commerce, Bureau of the Census. *Preliminary Review of Existing Studies of the Number of Illegal Residents in the United States.* Washington, D.C.: GPO, 1980.

————. Department of Justice. *Preliminary Report: Domestic Council Committee on Illegal Aliens.* Washington, D.C.: GPO, 1976.

————. Department of Justice. *Preliminary Report: Domestic Council Committee on Illegal Aliens.* Washington, D.C.: Dept. of Justice, December 1976.

————. General Accounting Office. *Problems and Options in Estimating the Size of the Illegal Alien Population.* Washington, D.C.: GPO, 1982.

VanArsdol, Maurice Jr. et al. *"Non-Apprehended and Apprehended Undocumented Residents in the Los Angeles Labor Market: An Exploratory Study."* Los Angeles: University of Southern California, 1978.

Vialet, Joyce. *Temporary Worker Programs: Background and Issues.* Washington, D.C.: Congressional Research Service, Library of Congress, 1980.

Wambaugh, Joseph. *Lines and Shadows.* New York: Morrow, 1984.

Weaver, Thomas and Theodore E. Downing, eds. *Mexican Migration.* Tucson: University of Arizona, Department of Anthropology, 1976.

Weintraus, Sidney and Stanley R. Ross. *"Temporary" Alien Workers in the U.S.: Designing Policy from Fact and Opinion.* Boulder, Colo.: Westview Press, 1982.

————. *The Illegal Alien from Mexico: Policy Choices for an Intractable Issue.* Austin: Mexico-United States Border Research Program, University of Texas at Austin, 1980.

Williams, Brett. *The Trip Takes Us: Chicano Migrants on the Prairie.* Master's Thesis, University of Illinois at Urbana-Champaign, 1975.

Articles

Alba, Francisco. "Mexico's International Migration as a Manifestation of Its Development Pattern." *International Migration Review.* 12 (Winter 1978): 502-513.

Bach, Robert Leroy. "Mexican Immigration and the American State." *International Migration Review.* 12 (Winter 1978): 536-555.

————. "Mexican Immigration and U.S. Immigration Reforms in the 1960s." *Kapitalistate.* 7(1978): 63-80.

Bean, Frank D., Harley L. Browning, and W. Parker Frisbie. "The Sociodemographic Characteristics of Mexican Immigrant Status Groups: Implications for Studying Undocumented Mexicans." *International Migration Review.* 18 (Fall 1984): 672-691.

Bean, Frank D., Allan G. King, and Jeffrey Passel. "The Number of Mexican Origin in the United States: Sex-Ratio-Based Estimates for 1980." *Demography* 20 (February 1983).

Bloom, Leonard. "Mexicans in the United States." *Sociology and Social Research* 36 (January-February 1952): 150-58.

Bogardus, Emory S. "Mexican Immigrants." *Sociology and Social Research* 11 (May-June 1927): 470-88.

————. "Mexican Immigrant and Segregation." *American Journal of Sociology* July 1930, 74-80.

————. "Second Generation Mexicans." 13 (January-February 1929): 276-83.

Borjas, George J. "The Labor Supply of Male Hispanic Immigrants in the United States." *International Migration Review* 17 (Winter 1983): 653-671.

Briggs, Vernon, Jr. "Methods of Analysis of Illegal Immigration into the United States." *International Migration Review* 18 (Fall 1984): 623-641.

Bullock, Paul. "Employment Problems of the Mexican-American." *Industrial Relations* May 1964, 37-50.

Buraway, Michael. "The Functions and Reproduction of Migrant Labor: Comparative Material From Southern Africa and the United States." *American Journal of Sociology* March 1976, 1050-1087.

Bustamante, Jorge A. "Structural and Ideological Conditions of Mexican Undocumented Immigration to United States." *American Behavioral Scientist* 19 (1976): 364-376.

————. "Undocumented Immigration From Mexico: Research Report." *International Migration Review* 11 (Summer 1977): 149-177.

Bustamante, Jorge A., and Geronimo G. Martinez. "Undocumented Immigration From Mexico: Beyond Borders But Within Systems." *Journal of International Affairs* 33(Fall/Winter 1979): 265-284.

"California Tries to Dam the Alien Tide." *Business Week* 12 February 1972.

Chapman, Leonard F. "'Silent Invasion' That Takes Millions of American Jobs." *U.S. News & World Report* 9 December 1974.

Chiswick, Barry R. "Illegal Aliens in the U.S. Labor Market." Proceedings of the International Economic Association 6th World Congress, 1984.

Corwin, Arthur F. "The Numbers Game: Estimates of Illegal Aliens in the United States, 1970-1981." *Law & Contemporary Problems* 4 (Spring 1982): 223-284.

Cuthbert, Richard W., and Joe B. Stevens. "The Net Economic Incentive for Illegal Mexican Migration: A Case Study." *International Migration Review* 15 (Fall 1981): 543-550.

Dagodag, Tim W. "Source Region and Composition of Illegal Mexican Immigration to California." *International Migration Review* 9 (Winter 1975): 499-511.

Dilmus, James D., and John S. Evans. "Conditions of Employment and Income Distribution in Mexico as Incentives for Mexican Migration to the United States: Prospects to the End of the Century." *International Migration Review* 13 (Spring 1979):

Downes, Richard. "The Future Consequences of Illegal Immigration." *The Futurist* 11 (1977): 125-127.

Ericson, Anna-Stina. "The Impact of Commuters on the Mexican-American Border Area." *Monthly Labor Review* August 1970.

Fallows, Marjorie. "The Mexican-American Laborers: A Different Drummer?" *Massachusetts Review* 8 (Winter 1967): 166-176.

Fernandez, Celestino and Lawrence R. Pedroza. "The Border Patrol and News Media Coverage of Undocumented Mexican Immigration During the 1970s: A Quantitative Content Analysis in the Sociology of Knowledge." *California Sociologist* 5 (Summer 1982): 1-26.

Fitzpatrick, Joseph P. "The Naturalization of Mexican Immigrants in the United States." *International Migration Review* 1 (Fall 1966): 5-16.

Fogel, Walter. "Illegal Alien Workers in the United States." *Industrial Relations* 16 (1977): 243-63.

―――. "Job Gains of Mexican-American Men." *Monthly Labor Review* October 1968, 22-27.

Frisbee, Parker W. "Illegal Migration From Mexico to the United States: A Longitudinal Analysis." *International Migration Review* (1975): 3-15.

Garcia, John A. "Political Integration of Mexican Immigrants: Explorations Into the Naturalization Process." *International Migration Review* (Winter 1981):

Gerking, Shelby D., and John G. Mutti. "Costs and Benefits of Illegal Immigration: Key Issues for Government Policy." *Social Science Quarterly* June 1980, 71-85.

Gorz, André. "Immigrant Labor." *New Left Review* 61 (May-June 1970): 28-31.

Graham, Otis. "Illegal Immigration and the New Reform Movement." *Immigration Papers II* (February 1980) Federation for American Immigration Reform.

Grebler, Leo. "The Naturalization of Mexican Immigrants in the United States." *International Migration Review* 1 (Fall 1966): 17-32.

Griffin, E. "The Real Immigration Reform-Help Mexican Workers at Home." *Nation* 238 (1984): 250-252.

Harwood, Edwin. "Arrests Without Warrant: The Legal and Organizational Environment of Immigration Law Enforcement." *UC Davis Law Review* 17 (Winter 1984): 520-525.

Heer, David M. "What is the Annual Net Flow of Undocumented Mexican Immigrants to the United States?" *Demography* August 1979, 417-423.

Hernandez, Jose, et al. "Census Data and the Problem of Conceptually Defining the Mexican-American Population." *Social Science Quarterly* March 1973, 671-687.

Hirschman, Charles. "Prior U.S. Residence Among Mexican Immigrants." *Social Forces* June 1978, 1179-1202.

"'Invasion' by Illegal Aliens and the Problems They Create." *U.S. News & World Report* 23 July 1973.

Jasso, Guillermina and Mark R. Rosenzweig. "Estimating the Emigration Rates of Legal Immigrants Using Administrative and Survey Data: The 1971 Cohort of Immigrants to the United States." *Demography* 19 (1982): 279-290.

Jenkins, J. Craig. "Push/Pull in Recent Mexican Migration to the U.S." *International Migration Review* 11 (Summer 1977): 178-189.

————. "The Demand for Immigrant Workers: Labor Scarcity or Social Control." *International Migration Review* 12 (Winter 1978): 514-535.

Kiser, George C. "Mexican American Labor Before World War II." *Journal of Mexican American History* 2 (1972).

Long, James E. "Productivity, Employment, Discrimination, and the Relative Economic Status of Spanish-Origin Males." *Social Science Quarterly* December 1977, 357-373.

Lopez, G.P. "Undocumented Mexican Migration—In Search of a Just Immigration Law and Policy." UCLA *Law Review* 28 (1981): 615-714.

Martin, Philip L., and Alan Richards. "International Migration of Labor: Boon or Bane?" *Monthly Labor Review* October 1980.

Massey, Douglas S., and Kathleen Schnabel. "Recent Trends in Hispanic Immigration to the U.S." *International Migration Review* 17 (Spring 1983): 212-244.

Mittelbach, Fran G., and Joan W. Moore. "Ethnic Endogamy—The Case of Mexican-American." *American Journal of Sociology* July 1968, 50-62.

Newman, Morris J. "A Profile of Hispanics in the U.S. Work Force." *Monthly Labor Review* December 1978, 3-14.

Penalosa, Fernando. "The Changing Mexican-American in Southern California." *Sociology and Social Research* July 1967, 405-417.

Portes, Alejandro. "Illegal Immigration and the International System, Lessons From Recent Legal Mexican Immigrants to the United States." *Social Problems* 26 (1979): 425-438.

————. "Toward a Structural Analysis of Illegal (Undocumented) Immigration." *International Migration Review* 12 (Winter 1978).

Reichart, Joshua S., and Douglas S. Massey. "Patterns of U.S. Migration From a Mexican Sending Community: A Comparison of Legal and Illegal Migrants." *International Migration Review* 13 (Winter 1979): 599-623.

Spalding, Rose J. "Mexican Immigration: A Historical Perspective." *Latin American Research Review* 18 (1983): 201-209.

Stoddard, Ellwyn R. "A Concept Analysis of the 'Alien Invasion': Institutionalized Support of Illegal Mexican Aliens in the U.S." *International Migration Review* 10 (Summer 1976): 157-186.

———. "Illegal Mexican Labor in the Borderlands: Institutionalized Support of an Unlawful Practice." *Pacific Sociological Review* April 1976, 175-210.

Thompson, G., R. Amon, and P.L. Martin. "Mexicans or Tomatoes— Immigration and Imports." *Journal of Policy Analysis & Management* 4 (1985): 603.

Wachter, Michael L. "Second Thoughts About Illegal Immigrants." *Fortune* 22 May 1978.

White, Franklin W. "Who Needs a Guestworker Program?" *Caribbean Review* 11 (Winter 1982).

Immigration and Ethnicity

Books

Alloway, David N., and Francesco Cordasco. *Minorities and the American City: A Sociological Primer for Educators*. New York: McKay, 1970.

Archdeacon, Thomas J. *Becoming American: An Ethnic History*. New York: Free Press; London: Collier Macmillan, 1983.

Berry, Brewton. *Race and Ethnic Relations*. Boston: Houghton, Mifflin, 1965.

Bogardus, Emory S. *Essentials of Americanization*. Los Angeles: University of Southern California Press, 1923.

———. *Immigration and Race Attitudes*. New York: D.C. Heath & Co., 1928.

Brown, Francis J., and Joseph S. Brown, eds. *One America: The History, Contributions and Present Problems of Our Racial and National Minorities*. New York: Prentice-Hall, 1952.

Claude, Inis. *National Minorities: An International Problem*. Cambridge, Mass.: Harvard University Press, 1958.

Cole, Stewart G., and Mildred W. Cole. *Minorities and the American Promise: The Conflict of Principle and Practice*. New York: Harper, 1954.

DeVos, George A. "Minority Group Identity." In *Culture Change, Mental Health and Poverty*. Edited by Joseph C. Finney. Lexington, Ky.: University of Kentucky Press, 1969.

Dinnerstein, Leon and David Reimers. *Ethnic Americans: A History of Immigration and Assimilation*. New York: Harper & Row, 1975.

Ethnic Groups in American Life. New York: Arno Press, 1978.

Fuchs, Lawrence H. *American Ethnic Politics*. New York: Harper & Row, 1968.

Gittler, Joseph B., ed. *Understanding Minority Groups*. New York: John Wiley, 1956.

Gordon, Milton M. *Assimilation in American Life: The Role of Race, Religion and National Origins*. Fairlawn, N.J.: Oxford University Press, 1964.

Greeley, Andrew M. *Ethnicity, Denomination, and Inequality.* Beverly Hills, Calif.: Sage, 1976.

———. *Ethnicity in the United States: A Preliminary Reconnaissance.* New York: Wiley, 1974.

———. "Immigration and Religion-Ethnic Group: A Sociological Reappraisal." In *The Gateway: U.S. Immigration Issues and Policies.* Edited by Barry R. Chiswick. Washington, D.C.: American Enterprise Institute, 1981.

Hartwell, Elizabeth Anne. "Cultural Assimilation, Social Mobility, and Persistence of Cognitive." Ph.D. Dissertation, Brandeis University, 1968.

Hawkins, Brett W., and Robert Lorenshas. *The Ethnic Factor in American Politics.* Columbus, Ohio: Merrill, 1970.

Hollingshead, August B. "Stratification in American Society." In *The Contribution of the Social Sciences to Psychotherapy.* Edited by L. Bernstein and B. Cullen Burris. Springfield, Ill.: Charles Thomas, 1967.

Huthmacher, J. *A Nation of Newcomers: Ethnic Minorities in American History.* New York: Dell Publishing Co., 1967.

Ignacio, Lemuel. *Asian Americans and Pacific Islanders: Is There Such an Ethnic Group?* San Jose, Calif.: Pilipino Development Associates, 1976.

Kinton, Jack, ed. *American Ethnic Revival.* Aurora, Ill.: Social Science and Sociological Resources, 1977.

Kramer, Judith R. *The American Minority Community.* New York: Thomas Y. Crowell, 1970.

Kramer, Judith R., and Seymour Leventman. *Children of the Gilded*

    Ghetto: Conflict Resolutions of Three Generation of American Jews. New Haven: Yale University Press, 1961.

Lenski, Gerhard E. *Power and Privilege: A Theory of Social Stratification.* New York: McGraw-Hill, 1966.

Levine, Edward M. *The Irish and Irish Politicians.* Notre Dame, Ind.: Notre Dame University Press, 1966.

Lieberson, Stanley. *Ethnic Patterns in American Cities.* New York: The Free Press of Glencoe, 1963.

Litt, Edgar. *Ethnic Politics in America: Beyond Pluralism.* Glenview, Ill.: Scott, Foresman, 1970.

Maldonado, Lionel and Joan Moore, eds. *Urban Ethnicity in the United States. New Immigrants and Old Minorities.* Urban Affairs Annual Reviews, Vol. 29. Beverly Hills, Calif.: Sage Publications, 1985.

Namazi, Kevan H. "Assimilation and Need Assessment Among Mexican, Cuban, and Middle Eastern Immigrants: A Multivariate Analysis." Ph.D. Dissertation, The University of Akron, 1984.

Parenti, Michael J. "Ethnic and Political Attitudes: A Depth Study of Italian Americans." Ph.D. Dissertation, Yale University, 1961.

Schermerhorn, R.A. *These Our People: Minorities in American Culture.* Boston: D.C. Heath, 1949.

Sherman, C. Bezalel. *The Jews Within American Society: A Study in Ethnic Individuality.* Detroit: Wayne State University Press, 1961.

Sowell, Thomas. *Ethnic America: A History.* New York: Basic, 1981.

Weyl, Nathaniel. *The Jew in American Politics.* New Rochelle, N.Y.: Arlington House, 1968.

Articles

Abramson, Harold J., and C. Edward Noll. "Religion, Ethnicity, and Social Change." *Review of Religious Research* 8 (Fall 1966): 11-26.

Archdeacon, Thomas J. "Problems and Possibilities in the Study of American Immigration and Ethnic History." International Migration Review 19 (Spring 1985): 112-134.

Bogardus, Emory S. "A Race-Relation Cycle." American Journal of Sociology January 1930, 612-17.

Bonacich, Edna. "A Theory of Ethnic Antagonism: The Split Labor Market." *American Sociological Review* October 1972, 547-559.

Cecci, Camillo. "Ethnic Identification in Second and Third Generation Emigrants." *Studi Emigrazione* June 1967, 209-252.

Curran, Thomas J. "Assimilation and Nativism." *International Migration Digest* 3 (Spring 1966): 15-25.

Duncan, Beverly and Otis Dudley Duncan. "Minorities and the Process of Stratification." *American Sociological Review* June 1968, 356-364.

Glazer, Daniel. "Dynamics of Ethnic Identification." *American Sociological Review* February 1958, 31-40.

Gordon, Milton M. "Assimilation in America: Theory and Reality." *Daedalus* 90 (Spring 1961): 263-285.

Greeley, Andrew M. "American Sociology and the Study of Ethnic Immigrant Groups." *International Migration Digest* 2 (Fall 1964): 107-113.

Halpern, Ben. "Ethnic and Religious Minorities: Subcultures and

Subcommunities." *Jewish Sociological Studies* January 1965, 37-44.

Handlin, Oscar, et. al. "Ethnic Groups in American Life." *Daedalus* (Spring 1961): 217-349.

Hirschman, Charles. "Immigrants and Minorities: Old Questions for New Direction in Research." *International Migration Review* 16 (Spring 1982): 474-490.

Katzman, M.T. "Discrimination, Subculture, and the Economic Performance of Negroes, Puerto Rican and Mexican-Americans." *American Journal of Economics and Sociology* 27 (1968): 371-5.

————. "Urban Racial Minorities and Immigrant Groups: Some Economic Comparisons." *American Journal of Economics and Sociology* January 1971, 15-26.

Lieberson, Stanley. "A Societal Theory of Race and Ethnic Relations." *American Sociological Review* December 1961, 902-910.

Light, Ivan. "Immigrant and Ethnic Enterprise in North America." *Ethnic and Racial Studies* 7 (1984):

Nahirny, Vladimir C., and Fishman, Joshua A. "American Immigrant Groups: Ethnic Identification and the Problem of Generation." *Sociological Review* November 1965, 311-326.

Nelli, Humbert S. "Italians in Urban America: A Study in Ethnic Adjustment." *International Migration Review* 1 (Summer 1967): 38-55.

Noel, Donald L. "A Theory of the Origin of Ethnic Stratification." *Social Problems* 16 (Fall 1968): 157-172.

Pavalko, R.M. "Racism and the New Immigration—A Reinterpretation of the Assimilation of White Ethnics in American Society." *Sociology and Social Research* 65 (1980): 56-77.

Roucek, Joseph S. "American Ethnic and Religious Minorities in America." *Politico* March 1959, 84-100.

————. "Special Characteristics of the Problem of Racial Minorities in the USA." *Revista Internacional de Sociologia* 25 (July-December 1967): 113-138.

Sherman, C. Bezalel. "Emerging Patterns and Attitudes in American Jewish Life." *Jewish Journal of Sociology* June 1963, 47-54.

Vecoli, R.J., and J. Rudolph. "Return to the Melting Pot: Ethnicity in the United States in the Eighties." *Siirtolaisuus-Migration* (1974-1984): 117-132.

New Immigration

<u>Books</u>

Alexander, Tom. "Those Amazing Cuban Emigrés." In *The Aliens: A History of Ethnic Minorities in America.* Edited by Leonard Dinnerstein and Frederic Cople Jaher. New York: Meredith, 1970.

Ariyabuddhiphongs, Vanchai. "A Test of Two Models of Need Hierarchy Theory Among Filipino Immigrants and Vietnamese Refugees." Ph.D. Dissertation, City University of New York, 1981.

Baker, R.P., and David S. North. *The 1975 Refugees: Their First Five Years in America.* Washington, D.C.: New TransCentury Foundation, 1984. Mimeo.

Birmingham, Stephen. *The Rest of Us: The Rise of America's Eastern European Jews.* New York: Berkeley Publishing Corp., 1985.

Boswell, Thomas D., and James R. Curtis. *The Cuban-American Experience: Culture, Images, and Perspectives.* Totowa, N.J.: Rowman and Allanheld, 1984.

Bryce-Laporte, Roy S., and Stephen R. Couch, eds. *Exploratory Fieldwork on Latino Migrants and Indochinese Refugees.* Washington, D.C.: RIIES Research Notes, No. 1, 1976.

Bryce-Laporte, Roy S., and Delores M. Mortimer. *Contemporary Studies of the Black Female and the Migratory Experience in the United States.* Washington: RIIE Research Notes, No. 3, n.d.

————, eds. *Caribbean Immigration to the United States.* Washington, D.C.: Research Institute on Immigration and Ethnic Studies (RIIES), Smithsonian Institute, 1976.

Burma, John H. *The Spanish-Speaking Groups in the United States.* Durham, N.C.: Duke University Press, 1954.

Cafferty, Pastora San Juan, et all. *The Dilemma of American Immigration: Beyond the Golden Door.* New Brunswick, N.J.: Transaction Books, 1983.

California Advisory Committee to U.S. Commission on Civil Rights. *Asian American and Pacific Peoples: A Case of Mistaken Identity.* Washington: GPO, 1975.

California Advisory Committee to U.S. Commission on Civil Rights. *A Dream Unfulfilled: Korean and Filipino Health Professionals in California.* Washington: GPO, 1975.

Casal, Lourdes. "Cubans in the United States: Their Impact on U.S.-Cuban Relations." In *Revolutionary Cuba in the World Arena.* Edited by Martin Weinstein. Philadelphia: ISHI, 1979.

Caudill, William A. *Japanese-American Personality and Acculturation.* Provincetown, Mass.: Journal Press, 1952.

Centro de Estudios Puertorriquenos. *Labor Migration Under Capitalism: The Puerto Rican Experience*. New York: Monthly Review Press, 1978.

Clark, Juan M. "The Exodus From Revolutionary Cuba (1959-1974): A Sociological Analysis." Ph.D. Dissertation, University of Florida, Gainesville, 1975.

Colakovic, Branko Mita. *Yugoslav Migrations to America*. San Francisco: R & E Research Associates, 1973.

Coolidge, Mary R. *Chinese Immigration*. New York: Arno Press, reprint, 1969.

Cordova, Fred. *Filipinos: The Forgotten Asian Americans*. Seattle: Demonstration Project for Asian Americans, 1983.

Cornelius, Wayne A. *America in the Era of Limits: Nativists' Reaction to the "New" Immigration*. La Jolla: Center for U.S.-Mexican Studies, University of California, San Diego

Crewdson, John. *The Tarnished Door: The New immigrants and the Transformation of America*. New York: Times Books, 1983.

Cuddy, D.L., ed. *Contemporary American Immigration: Interpretive Essays (European). Contemporary American Immigration: Interpretive Essays (Non-European)*. Boston: Twayne Publishers, 1982.

Davie, Maurice Rea. *World Immigration With Special Reference to the U.S.* New York: The Macmillan Co., 1936.

Day, Carol O., and Edmund Day. *New Immigrants*. Denbury, Conn.: Watts, 1985.

Easterlin, Richard A. "Economic and Social Characteristics of the Immigrants." In *Immigration*. Edited by R. Easterlin, D. Ward,

W.S. Bernard, and R. Veda. Cambridge, Mass.: Belknap Press, 1980.

Elkholy, Abdo. *Arab Moslems in the United States: Religion and Assimilation*. New Haven, Conn.: College and University Press, 1966.

Fairchild, Henry P. *The Melting Pot Mistake*. Boston: Little, Brown & Co., 1926.

Fawcett, J.T., et. al. *Asia Pacific Immigration to the United States*. Honolulu: East-West Population Institute, 1985.

Fitzpatrick, Joseph P. *Puerto Rican Americans: The Meaning of Migration to the Mainland*. Englewood Cliffs, N.J.: Prentice-Hall, 1971.

Fuchs, Lawrence H. et. al. *Should United States Immigration Policy Be Changed?* Washington, D.C.: American Enterprise Institute, 1980.

Gans, Herbert J. *The Urban Villagers: Group and Class in the Life of Italian Americans*. New York: Free Press, 1962.

Govorchin, Gerald Gilbert. *Americans from Yugoslavia*. Gainesville: University of Florida Press, 1961.

Grant, Bruce. *The Boat People*. New York: Penguin Books, 1980.

Greeley, Andrew M. *The American Catholic: A Social Portrait*. New York: Basic Books, 1977.

Guiness, Paul and Michael Bradshaw. *North America: A Human Geography*. Totowa, N.J.: Barnes & Noble, 1985.

Hagopian, Elaine C., ed. *The Arab-Americans: Studies in Assimilation*. Wilmette, Ill.: Medina University Press International, 1969.

Handlin, Oscar. *The American People in the Twentieth Century*. Boston: Beacon Press, 1963.

————. "Immigration in American Life: A Reappraisal." In *Immigration and American History*. Edited by H.S. Commanger. Minneapolis: University of Minnesota Press, 1961.

————. *The Newcomers: Negroes and Puerto Ricans in a Changing Metropolis*. Cambridge, Mass.: Harvard University Press, 1959.

————. *The Uprooted*. The Uprooted: The Epic Story of the Great Migrations that Made the American People. Boston: Little, Brown, 1951 or 1973.

Hansen, Marcus Lee. *The Immigrant in American History*. Cambridge, Mass.: Harvard University Press, 1940.

————. *The Problem of the Third Generation Immigrant*. Rock Island, Ill.: Augustana Historical Society, 1938.

Harper, Elizabeth. *Who are Today's Immigrants*. New York: American Immigration and Citizenship Conference, 1969.

Henkin, Alan B. *Between Two Countries: The Vietnamese in America*. Saratoga, Calif.: Century Twenty One Pub., 1981.

Herberg, Will. *Protestant-Catholic-Jew*. Garden City, N.Y.: Doubleday, 1955.

Hernandez, Andres R., ed. *The Cuban Minority in the U.S.: Final Report on Need Identification and Program Evaluation*. Washington, D.C.: Cuban National Planning Council, 1974.

Higham, John. *Send These to Me: Immigrants in Urban America*. Baltimore, Md.: The John Hopkins University Press, 1984.

Hsu, Francis L.K. *The Challenge of the American Dream*. Belmont, Calif.: Wadsworth, 1971.

Hurh, Won M. *"Comparative Study of Korean Immigrants in the United States: A Typological Approach."* San Francisco: R & E Research Associates, 1977.

Illsoo, Kim. *New Urban Immigrants: The Korean Community in New York*. Princeton: Princeton University Press, 1981.

The Indochinese, New Americans. Provo, Utah: The Center, 1981.

Jones, Maldwyn Allen. *American Immigration*. Chicago: University of Chicago Press, 1960.

Keely, Charles, et. al. *Profiles of Undocumented Aliens in New York City: Haitians and Dominicans*. New York: Center for Migration Studies, 1977.

Kelly, Gail Paradise. *From Vietnam to America*. Boulder, Colo.: Westview Press, 1977.

Kim, Bok-Lim C. *The Asian Americans: Changing Patterns, Changing Needs*. Montclair, N.J.: Association of Korean Christian Scholars in North America, 1978.

Kim, Hyung-Chan and Wayne Patterson, eds. *The Koreans in America, 1882-1974*. Dobbs Ferry, N.Y.: Oceana, 1974.

Kim, Illsoo. *New Urban Immigrants: The Korean Community in New York*. Princeton, N.J.: Princeton University Press, 1981.

Kim, Warren Y. *Koreans in America*. Los Angeles: Po Chin Chai, 1971.

Kitano, Harry H.L. *Japanese Americans*. 2nd ed. Englewood Cliffs, N.J.: Prentice-Hall, 1976.

Kolm, Richard. "The Change of Cultural Identity: An Analysis of Factors Conditioning the Cultural Integration of Immigrants." Ph.D. Dissertation, Wayne State University, 1967.

Kubat, Daniel. *The Politics of Migration Policies*. New York: Center for Migration Studies, 1979.

Lamm, Richard D., and Gary Imhoff. *Immigration Time Bomb: The Fragmenting of America*. Dutton, 1985.

Laska, Vera. *The Czechs in America, A Chronology and Fact Book, 1633-1977*. Dobbs Ferry, N.Y.: Oceana, 1977.

Lasker, Bruno. *Filipino Immigration*. New York: Arno Press, 1969.

Lasker, Bruno. *Filipino Immigration to Continental United States and to Hawaii*. Chicago: University of Chicago Press, 1931.

Lee, Rose Hum. *The Chinese in the United States of America*. Hong Kong: Hong Kong University Press, 1960.

Llanes, José. *Cuban Americans: Masters of Survival*. Cambridge, Mass.: ABT, 1982.

Lyman, Stanford. *Chinese Americans*. New York: Random House, 1974.

Mark, Diane Mei Lin and Ginger Chih. *A Place Called Chinese America*. Dubuque, Iowa: Kendall/Hunt Publishing Co., 1932.

Marshall, F. Ray. *Illegal Immigration: The Problem, The Solutions*. Washington, D.C.: Federation for American Immigration Reform, 1982.

Meadows, Paul, et. al. *Recent Immigration to the United States: The Literature of the Social Sciences*. Washington, D.C.: Smithsonian

Institution Research Institute on Immigration and Ethnic Studies, 1976.

Miller, Jake C. *The Plight of Haitian Refugees*. New York: Praeger, 1984.

Montero, Darrel. *Vietnamese Americans*. Boulder, Colo.: Western Press, 1979.

————. *Vietnamese Americans: Patterns of Resettlement and Socioeconomic Adaption in the U.S.* Boulder, Colo.: Westview Press, 1979.

Montero, Darrel and Marsha I. Weber. *Vietnamese Americans: Patterns of Resettlement and Sociological Adaptation in the United States.* Boulder, Colo.: Westview Press, 1979.

Moore, Joan and Harry Pachon. *Hispanics in the United States*. Englewood Cliffs, N.J.: Prentice-Hall, Inc., 1985.

Morris, Milton D. *Immigration—The Beleaguered Bureaucracy*. Washington, D.C.: Brookings Institution, 1985.

Muller, Thomas. *The Fourth Wave: California's Newest Immigrants*. Washington, D.C.: Urban Institute Press, 1984.

Naff, Alixia. *Becoming American: The Early Arab Immigrant Experience*. Carbondale, Ill.: Southern University Press, 1985 or 1986.

National Academy of Sciences. *Immigration Statistics: A Story of Neglect*. Washington: National Academy Press, 1985.

Papademetrion, Demetrios and Nicholas Dimarzio. *Profiling Unapprehended Undocumented Aliens in the New York Metropolitan Area: An Exploratory Study*. Interim Report, Center for Migration Studies, N.Y., 1982.

Parmet, Robert D. *Labor and Immigration in Industrial America*. Boston, Mass.: G.K. Hall, 1981.

Pedraza-Bailey, Silvia. *Political and Economic Migrants in America: Cubans and Mexicans*. Austin, Tex.: University of Texas Press, 1985.

Petersen, William. *Japanese-Americans*. New York: Random House, 1971.

Pido, Antonio J.A. *The Pilipinos in America*. New York: Center for Migration Studies, 1986.

Poston, Dudley L., Jr., Walter T. Martin, and Jerry D. Goodman. *The Socioeconomic Patterns of the New Immigrants to the United States. Does Increased Visibility Mean Decreased Opportunities?* Austin: University of Texas, Department of Sociology, 1978.

Prohias, Rafael J., and Lourdes Casal. *The Cuban Minority in the U.S.: Preliminary Report on Need Identification and Program Evaluation*. Boca Raton: Florida Atlantic University, 1973.

Propic, George J. *The Croatian Immigrants in America*. New York: Philosophical Library, 1971.

Reid, Ira de A. *The Negro Immigrant: His Background, Characteristics and Social Adjustment, 1899-1937*. New York: Arno Press and *The New York Times*, 1969.

Reimers, David M. *Still the Golden Door: The Third World Comes to America*. Columbia University Press, 1985.

Reubens, Edwin. *Temporary Admission of Foreign Workers: Dimensions and Policies*. Washington, D.C.: National Commission for Manpower Policy, 1979.

Roberts, Peter. *The New Immigration*. New York: Arno Press, 1970.

Rogg, Eleanor Meyer. *The Assimilation of Cuban Exiles: The Role of Community and Class*. New York: Aberdeen, 1974.

Rosenblum, Gerald. *Immigrant Workers: Their Impact on American Labor Radicalism*. New York: Basic Books, Inc., 1973.

————. "Modernization, Immigration, and the American Labor Movement." Ph.D. Dissertation, Princeton University, 1968.

Runblom, Harald and Hans Norman, eds. *From Sweden to America: A History of the Migration*. Minneapolis: University of Minnesota Press, 1976.

Saloutos, Theodore. *The Greeks in the United States*. Cambridge, Mass.: Harvard University Press, 1964.

Schwartz, Abba P. *The Open Society*. New York: William Morrow & Co., 1968.

Senate Committee on the Judiciary, Subcommittee on Immigration. *The West Indies (BWI) Temporary Alien Labor Program: (1943-1977)*. GPO, 1978.

Shannon, William V. *The American Irish*. New York: Macmillan, 1964.

Siegal, Jacob S., Jeffrey S. Passel, and J. Gregory Robinson. *Preliminary Review of Existing Studies of the Number of Illegal Residents in the United States*. Prepared for the U.S. Bureau of Census. Washington, D.C., January 1980. Mimeo.

Simon, Rita J. *Public Opinion and the Immigrant: Print Media Coverage, 1880-1980*. Lexington, Mass.: D.C. Heath & Co., 1985.

Strong, Edward K. *The Second Generation Japanese Problem*. Stanford: Stanford University Press, 1934.

Sullivan, Teresa A., and Silvia Pedraza-Bailey. *Differential Success Among Cuban-American and Mexican-American Immigrants: The Role of Policy and Community*. Washington: National Technical Information Service, 1979.

Swierenga, Robert P., ed. *The Dutch in America: Immigration, Settlement, and Cultural Change*. New Brunswick, N.J.: Rutgers University Press, 1985.

Tachiki, Amy, Eddie Wong, and Franklin Odo, eds. *Roots: An Asian American Reader*. Los Angeles: University of California, Los Angeles, Asian American Studies Center, 1971.

Taft, Donald R., and Richard Robbins. *International Migrations: The Immigrant in the Modern World*. New York: Ronald Press Co., 1955.

Taft, Julia V., et. al. *Refugee Resettlement in the U.S.: Time for a New Focus*. Washington: New Transcentury Fund, 1979.

Tomasi, Silvano M., and Madelaine Engel, eds. *The Italian Experience in the United States*. Staten Island, N.Y.: Center for Migration Studies, 1970.

Tomasi, Silvano M., and Charles B. Keely. *Whom Have We Welcomed?: The Adequacy and Quality of U.S. Immigration Data for Policy Analysis and Evaluation*. Staten Island, N.Y.: Center for Migration Studies, 1975.

United States. Commission on Civil Rights. *The Tarnished Door: Civil Rights Issues in Immigration*. (A Report of the United States Commission on Civil Rights, September 1980) Washington, D.C.: GPO, 1980.

————. Congress. House. Committee on Education and Labor, Subcommittee on Equal Opportunities. *Koreans in Los Angeles:*

Employment and Education, Hearings on H.R. 9895. 93 Cong., 2nd sess., 1974.

—————. —————. —————. Select Committee on Population. *Legal and Illegal Immigration to the United States.* Washington, D.C.: GPO, 1978.

—————. Immigration Commission. *Reports of the Immigration Commission.* Washington, D.C.: GPO, 1911.

University of Miami, Center for Advanced International Studies. *The Cuban Immigration 1959-1966 and its Impact on Miami-Dade County, Florida.* Coral Gables: University of Miami, 1967.

Vernant, Jacques. *The Refugee in the Post-War World.* New Haven: Yale University Press, 1953.

Wain, Barry. *The Refused.* New York: Simon and Schuster, 1981.

Williams, Jerry R. *And Yet They Come: Portuguese Immigration from the Azores to the United States.* New York: Center for Migration Studies, 1982.

Wittke, Carl Frederick. *The Irish in America.* Baton Rouge: Louisiana State University Press, 1956.

Ziegler, B.M., ed. *Immigration: An American Dilemma.* Boston: D.C. Heath, 1953.

Articles

Bach, Robert L. "The Cuban Exodus." *Caribbean Review* 11 (Winter 1982).

—————. "The New Cuban Immigrants: Their Background and Prospects." *Monthly Labor Review* October 1980, 39-46.

Bach, Robert L., Jennifer B. Bach, and Timothy Triplett. "The Flotilla Entrants': Latest and Most Controversial." *Cuban Studies* 11/12 (July 1981/January 1982): 29-48.

Barnett, Milton L. "Kinship as a Factor Affecting Cantonese Economic Adaptation in the United States." *Human Organization* 19 (Spring 1960): 40-46.

Befu, Harumi. "Contrastive Acculturation of California Japanese." *Human Organization* 24 (Fall 1965): 209-216.

Bernard, William S. "The Integration of Immigrants in the United States." *International Migration Review* 1 (Spring 1967): 23-32.

Birks, J.S., and C.A. Sinclair. "Migration and Development: The Changing Perspective of the Poor Arab Countries." *Journal of International Affairs* 33 (Fall/Winter 1979): 285-309.

Bisharat, Mary. "Yemeni Farmworkers in California." *Middle East Research & Information Reports* January 1975, 22-26.

Black, Isabella. "American Labour and Chinese Immigration." *Past and Present* July 1963, 59-76.

Bloch, Louis. "Occupations of Immigrants Before and After Coming to the United States." *Journal of the American Statistical Association* 17 (1921): 750-64.

Boyd, Monica. "The Changing Nature of Central and Southeast Asian Immigration to the United States: 1961-1972." *International Migration Review* 8(Winter 1974): 507-519.

————. "Oriental Immigration: The Experience of the Chinese, Japanese, and Filipino Population in the United States." *International Migration Review* 5,1 (Spring 1971).

Bouvier, Leon S. "International Migration: Yesterday, Today, and Tomorrow." *Population Bulletin* September 1977,

Bryce-Laporte, Roy Simon. "Black Immigrants." *Journal of Black Studies* September 1972, 29-56.

———. "Dreams and Destinations: The Caribbean Immigrant in the United States." Remarks Delivered Before the United States House of Representatives, Subcommittee on Inter-American Affairs, September 10 and 21, 193. Reprinted in *Continuities.* New York: State University of New York, Black Studies Department, Spring 1975.

———. "Visibility of the New Immigrants." *Society* 14 (September/ October 1977): 18-33.

Burma, John H. "The Background of the Current Situation for Filipino-Americans." *Social Forces* October 1951, 42-48.

Casal, Lourdes and Andres R. Hernandez. "Cubans in the U.S.: A Survey of the Literature." *Cuban Studies* July 1975, 25-31.

Chiswick, Barry R. "An Analysis of the Earnings and Employment of Asian-American Men." *Journal of Labor Economics* April 1983.

Choy, Philip P. "Golden Mountain of Lead: The Chinese Experience in California." *California Historical Quarterly* September 1970, 267-276.

Chyz, Jaroslav and Joseph S. Roucek. "The Russians in the United States." *The Slavonic and East European Review* 17 (1939): 638-658.

Cuddy, Edward. "Irish-Americans and the 1961 Election: An Episode in Immigrant Adjustment." *American Quarterly* XXI (Summer 1969): 228-243.

Daniels, Roger. "American Historians and East Asian Immigrants." *Pacific Historical Review* November 1974, 449-472.

————. "Westerners from the East: Oriental Immigrants Reappraised." *Pacific Historical Review* November 1966, 373-383.

Diaz-Briquets, Sergio. "Demographic and Related Determinants of Recent Cuban Emigration." *International Migration Review* 17 (Spring to Winter 1983): 95-119.

Douglas, Paul A. "Is the New Immigration More Unskilled than the Old?" *Publications of the American Statistical Association* 26 (1918-1919): 393-403.

Drora, Kass and Seymour Martin Lipset. "America's New Wave of Jewish Immigrants." *New York Times Sunday Magazine* 7 December 1980.

Eckerson, Helen F. "Immigration and National Origins." *The Annals of the American Academy of Political and Social Science* September 1966, 4-14.

Fallows, James. "The New Immigrants." *The Atlantic* November 1983.

Finck, John. "The Indochinese in America: Progress Toward Self-Sufficiency." *World Refugee Survey* (1983): 56-59.

Fong, Stanley L.M. "Assimilation of Chinese in America: Changes in Orientation and Social Perception." *American Journal of Sociology* March 1965, 265-273.

Fornard, Robert J. "Asian-Indians in America: Acculturation and Minority Status." *Migration Today* 12 (1984); 28-32.

Fortney, Judith. "Immigrant Professionals: A Brief Historical Survey." *International Migration Review* 1 (1972):

Fox, Geoffrey E. "Cuban Workers in Exile." *Trans-Action* September 1971, 21-30.

Fuchs, Lawrence H. "Some Political Aspects of Immigration." *Law and Contemporary Problems* 21 (Spring 1956): 270-283.

Gordon, Linda W. "Settlement Patterns of Indochinese Refugees in the United States." *INS Reporter* (Spring 1980): 8-10.

Graham, O.L. "The New Immigration." *Dissent* 28 (1981): 127-128.

Gugler, Joseph. "A Minimum of Urbanism and a Maximum of Ruralism: The Cuban Experience." *Studies in Comparative International Development* 15 (Summer 1980): 27-44.

Hansen, Marcus L. "The History of American Immigration as a Field for Research." *American Historical Review* April 1927, 500-518.

Harwood, Edwin. "Alienation: American Attitudes Toward Immigration." *Public Opinion* (June/July 1983): 49-51.

Heiss, Jerold. "Factors Related to Immigrant Assimilation: The Early Post-Migration Situation." *Human Organization* 26 (Winter 1967): 265-272.

Hirschman, Charles and Morrison G. Wong. "Trends in Socioeconomic Achievements Among Immigrant and Native-Born Asian Americans, 1960-1976." *The Sociological Quarterly* 22 (Autumn 1981): 485-523.

Hohl, Donald G. "The Indochinese Refugee: The Evolution of United States Policy." *International Migration Review* 12 (Spring 1978): 128-132.

Hossain, Mokkerom. "South Asians in Southern California: A Sociological Study of Immigrants from India, Pakistan and Bangladesh." *South Asia Bulletin* 2 (1982): 74-83.

Houchins, Lee and Chang-So Houchins. "The Korean Experience in America, 1903-1924." *Pacific Historical Review* 43 (1974).

"Immigration and the Randomness of Ethnic Mix." *New York Times* 3 October 1984.

Jenson, J.M. "Apartheid: Pacific Coast Style." *Pacific Historical Review* August 1969, 335-340.

Keely, Charles B. "Immigration Composition and Population Policy." *Science* 185 (1974): 587-583.

————. "Philippine Migration: International Movements and the Emigration to the United States." *International Migration Review* (Summer 1972): 177-87.

Kim, Hyung-Chan. "Some Aspects of Social Demography of Korean Americans." *International Migration Review* 8 (Spring 1974):

Kitano, Harry H.L. "Asian Americans: The Chinese, Japanese, Koreans, Pilipinos, and Southeast Asians." *The Annals of the American Academy of Political and Social Sciences* 454 (1981).

Kollmann, Wolfgang and Peter Marschalck. "German Emigration to the United States." *Perspectives in American History* 7 (1973): 499-557.

Lamm, Richard D. "America Needs Fewer Immigrants." *New York Times Magazine*, 12 July 1981.

Lee, Robert. "Acculturation of Chinese Americans." *Sociology and Social Research* 36 (May-June 1952): 319-21.

Lee, Rose Hum. "The Chinese Abroad." *Phylon*, October 1956, 257-70.

Letman, Sloan T. and Francis G. Spranza. "Some Sociological Per spectives on the Immigration Problem." *Journal of Humanics*, December 1978, 107-121.

Lewthwaite, Gordon R., Christine Mainzer, and Patrick J. Holland. "From Polynesia to California: Samoan Migration and Its Sequel." *Journal of Pacific History* 8 (1973): 133-157.

Lindsey, Robert. "The New Asian Immigrants." *New York Times Magazine*, 9 May 1982, 22-28.

Lyman, Stanford M. "Contrasts in the Community Organization of Chinese and Japanese in North America." *Canadian Review of Sociology and Anthropology* 5 (May 1968): 51-67.

Massey, Douglas S. "Dimensions of the New Immigration to the United States and the Prospects for Assimilation." *Annual Review of Sociology* 7 (1981): 57-85.

McKenna, Marian G. "The Melting Pot: Comparative Observations in the United States and Canada." *Sociology and Social Research* 53 (July 1969):433-447.

Midgley, Elizabeth. "Immigrants: Whose Huddled Masses?" *Atlantic Monthly*, April 1978.

Modell, J. "Class or Ethnic Solidarity: The Japanese-American Company Union." *Pacific Historical Review* 38 (May 1969): 193-206.

Montgomery, Paul. "For Cuban Refugees, Promise of U.S. Fades." *New York Times Magazine*, 19 April 1981.

Mott, Frank L. "The Immigrant Worker." *Annual of the American Academy of Political and Social Science* 367 (September 1966): 23-32.

Moynihan, Daniel Patrick. "The Irish of New York." *Commentary*, August 1963, 93-107.

Munoz, Faye Untalan. "Pacific Islanders: A Perplexed, Neglected Minority." *Church and Society* (January-February 1974): 15-23.

Murphy, Ruth and Sonia Blumenthal. "The American Community and the Immigrant." *Annual of the American Academy of Political and Social Science* 367 (September 1966): 115-126.

New Immigrant Wave. "The New Immigrant Wave." *RIIES: Society Magazine* September/October 1977.

North, Hart H. "Chinese and Japanese Immigration to the Pacific Coast." *California Historical Society Quarterly* 28 (December 1949): 343-350.

Palmer, Ransford W. "A Decade of West Indian Migration to the United States; 1962-1972: An Economic Analysis." *Social and Economic Studies*, September 1974.

Pedraza-Bailey, Sylvia. "Cuba's Exiles: Portrait of a Refugee Migration." *International Migration Review* 19 (Spring 1985): 4-34.

Peterson, William. "International Migration." *Annual Review of Sociology* 4 (1978): 533-575.

Portes, Alejandro and Rafael Mozo. "The Political Adaptation of Cubans and Other Ethnic Minorities in the United States: A Preliminary Analysis." *International Migration Review* 19 (Spring 1985): 55-63.

Portes, Alejandro, Juan M. Clark, and Robert L. Bach. "The New Wave: A Statistical Profile of Recent Cuban Exiles to the United States." *Cuban Studies*, January 1977, 1-32.

Power, Jonathan. "The Great Debate on Illegal Immigration." *Journal of International Affairs* 33 (Fall/Winter 1979):

Reubens, Edwin. "Aliens, Jobs, and Immigration Policy." *The Public Interest* 51 (1978): 113-134.

Rojo, T.A. "Social Maladjustment Among Filipinos in the United States." *Sociology and Social Research* 21 (May-June 1936): 447-57.

Rose, Peter I. "From Southeast Asia to America." *Migration Today* 9 (1981): 22-28.

————. "Links in a Chain: Observation of the American Refugee Program in Southeast Asia." *Migration Today* 9 (1981): 6-24.

————. "Some Reflections on Refugee Policy." *Dissent* (Fall 1984): 484-86.

Schermerhorn, R.A. "Minorities: European and American." *Phylon* 20 (Summer 1959): 178-185.

Shannon, Lyle W. "The Economic Absorption and Cultural Integration of Immigrant Workers." *American Behavioral Scientist*, September 1969, 36-56.

Siu, C.P. "The Sojourner." *American Journal of Sociology*, July 1952, 34-44.

Smith, Joel and Allan Kornberg. "Some Considerations Bearing Upon Comparative Research in Canada and the United States." *Sociology*, September 1969, 541-358.

Smith, Richard Ferree. "Refugees." *Annals of the American Academy of Political and Social Sciences* 367 (September 1966): 43-52.

Smither, Robert and Marta Rodriguez-Giegling. "Personality, Demographics, and Acculturation of Vietnamese and Nicaraguan Refugees to the United States." *International Journal of Psychology*, March 1982, 19-25.

Stern, Lewis M. "Response to Vietnamese Refugees: Surveys of Public Opinion." *Social Work*, July 1981, 306-311.

Tenhala, John. "Boat People Flee Haiti to U.S." In *1980 World Refugee Survey*. New York: U.S. Committee for Refugees, 1980.

Thomas, John F. "Cuban Refugees in the United States." *International Migration Review* 2 (Spring 1967): 46-57.

————. "Cuban Refugee Program." *Welfare in Review*, September 1963, 1-20.

Tyree, Adrea and Katherine Donato. "The Sex Composition of Legal Immigrants to the United States." *Sociology and Social Research*, July 1985, 577-585.

Velikonja, Joseph. "Italian Immigrants in the United States in the Mid-Sixties." *International Migration Review*, September 1967, 25-37.

Wain, Barry. "The Indochina Refugee Crises." *Foreign Affairs* (Fall 1979):

Watson, Hilbourne A. "West Indians in the United States—Why So Many?" *Amsterdam News*, 2 October 1976.

Wilke, Arthur S., and Raj P. Mohan. "The Politics of Asian Americans: An Assessment." *International Journal of Contemporary Sociology* 21 (July and October 1984): 28-71.

Wiseman, J.P. "Individual Adjustments and Kin Relationships in the New Immigration—An Approach to Research." *International Migration* 23 (1985): 348-68.

Wong, Paul. "The Emergence of the Asian American Movement." *The Bride* 2 (1972): 32-39.

Yu, Eui-Young. "A Comment on the Number of Koreans in 1970 U.S. Census of Population." *Korean Student Association of Southern California*, 1974.

Zeisel, Hans. "The Race Question in American Immigration." *Social Research*, June 1949, 222-29.

Zenner, Walter P. "Arab-Speaking Immigrants in North America as Middleman Minorities." *Ethnic and Racial Studies* 5 (1982): 457-77.

Zolberg, Aristide. "International Migration Policies in a Changing World System." In *Human Migration: Patterns and Policies*. Edited by William H. McNeill and Ruth S. Adams. Bloomington: Indiana University Press, 1978.

Impact of Immigration

<u>Books</u>

Bouvier, Leon S. *Immigration and its Impact on U.S. Society*. Washington, D.C.: Population Reference Bureau, 1981.

————. "The Impact of Immigration on United States Population Size." *Population Trends and Public Policy* Washington, D.C.: Population Reference Bureau, 1981.

Bryce-Laporte, Roy S., ed. with assistance of Delores M. Mortimer and Stephen R. Couch. *Sourcebook on the New Immigration: Implications for the United States and the International Community*. New Brunswick, N.J.: Transaction Books, 1979.

————. *Sourcebook on the New Immigration: Book II (Supplement)*. Washington, D.C.: Research Institute on Immigration and Ethnic Studies, Smithsonian Institute, 1979.

Chiswick, Barry R. *An Analysis of the Economic Progress and Impact of Immigrants.* Report Prepared Under Contract no. 21-06-78-20. Employment and Training Administration, U.S. Dept. of Labor, Mimeo (NTIS PB80-200454), 1980.

————. "The Economic Progress of Immigrants: Some Apparently Universal Patterns." In *Contemporary Economic Problem, 1979.* Edited by William Fellner. Washington: American Enterprise Institute, 1979.

————. *The Employment of Immigrants in the United States.* Washington, D.C.: American Enterprise Institute, 1983.

Community Research Associates (San Diego, California). *Undocumented Immigrants: Their Impact on the County of San Diego.* San Diego: Community Research Associates, 1980.

Cornelius, Wayne A. *America in the Era of Limits: Migrants, Nativists, and the Future of U.S.-Mexican Relations.* La Jolla, Calif.: Center for U.S.-Mexican Studies, University of California, San Diego, 1982.

————. *The Future of Mexican Immigrants in California: A New Perspective for Public Policy [With Special Reference to Health Care].* La Jolla, Calif.: Program in U.S.-Mexican Studies, University of California, San Diego, 1980.

————. *Immigration, Mexican Development Policy and the Future of U.S.-Mexican Relations.* La Jolla, Calif.: Program in U.S.-Mexican Studies, University of California, San Diego, 1981.

————. *The Future of Mexican Immigrants in California: A New Perspective for Public Publicy [i.e. Policy]* La Jolla, Calif.: Program in U.S.-Mexican Studies, University of California, San Diego, 1981.

————. *Mexican Migration to the United States: Causes, Consequences*

and U.S. Responses. Cambridge: Migration and Development
Study Group, Center for International Studies, M.I.T., 1978.

Corwin, Arthur F., ed. *Immigrants—and Immigrants: Perspectives on
Mexican Labor Migration to the United States.* Westport, Conn.:
Greenwood Press, 1978.

County Research Unit on Illegal Aliens County of San Diego Human
Resources Agency. *A Study of the Socioeconomic Impact of Illegal
Aliens on the County of San Diego.* San Diego: County of San
Diego Human Resources Agency, 1977.

Craig, Ann L. *Mexican Immigration: Changing Terms of the Debate in the
U.S. and Mexico:* Summary of a Briefing Session Sponsored by
the International Relations Division, the Rockefeller Foundation; Organized by the Program in U.S.-Mexican Studies, University of California, San Diego, June 10-12, 1979. La Jolla,
Calif.

Cross, Harry E., and James A. Sandos. *The Impact of Undocumented
Mexican Workers on the U.S.: A Critical Assessment.* Washington,
D.C.: Battelle Population and Development Policy Program,
1979.

Erb, Mary Elizabeth. *While America Sleeps, Foundations Crumble.*
Washington, D.C.: Goetz Co. Press, 1966.

Hill, Peter J. "Economic Impact of Immigration into the United
States." Ph.D. Dissertation, University of Chicago, 1970.

Ramirez, Armando Hipolito. "The Socioeconomic Impact of the
Illegal Aliens on the County of San Diego." Master's Thesis, San
Diego State University, 1976.

United States. Comptroller General of the United States Report to
the Congress. *Central American Refugees: Regional Conditions*

and Prospects and Potential Impact on the United States. Gaithersburg, Md.: GAO, July 20, 1984. Mimeo.

Williams, Dean L. *Some Political and Economic Aspects of Mexican Immigration Into the U.S. Since 1941; With Particular Reference to this Immigration into the State of California.* San Francisco: R & E Research Associates, 1973.

Articles

Bodnar, J.E. "Impact of New Immigration on Black Workers—Steelton, Pennsylvania, 1880-1920." *Labor History* 17 (1976): 214-229.

Cornelius, Wayne A. . "Building the Cactus Curtain: Mexican Immigration and U.S. Responses." Paper Prepared for the Latin American Program of the Woodrow Wilson International Center for Scholars, Washington, D.C., September 1979.

Fallows, James. "Immigration: How It's Affecting Us." *Atlantic Monthly* November 1983.

Gibson, Campbell. "The Contribution of Immigration to U.S. Population Growth: 1790-1970." *International Migration Review* 9 (1975): 157-177.

Keely, Charles B. "Effects of U.S. Immigration Laws on Manpower Characteristics of Immigrants." *Demography* May 1975, 179-191.

———. "Effects of the Immigration Act of 1965 on Selected Population Characteristics of Immigrants to the United States." *Demography* May 1971, 157-169.

Reder, Melvin W. "The Economic Consequences of Increased Immigration." *Review of Economics and Statistics* August 1963, 221-230.

Rivera-Batiz, Francisco. "The Effects of Immigration in a Distorted Two-Section Economy." *Economic Inquiry* 19 (1981):

Spengler, Joseph J. "Some Economic Aspects of Immigration into the United States." *Journal of Law and Contemporary Problems* 21 (Spring 1956): 236-265.

Usher, Dan. "Public Property and the Effects of Migration Upon Other Residents of the Migrant's Countries of Origin and Destination." *Journal of Political Economy* October 1977, 1001-1020.